"If you feel spiritually single as you seek to raise children who follow biblical principles, this book is for you! It addresses the challenging family issues you face and offers strategies for success that are practical and effective. Filled with real-life questions and answers that offer hope to the Christian spouse who has a marriage partner not walking with God, this book should also be in the hands of every Christian leader."

—CAROL KENT, speaker; author of *When I Lay My Isaac Down*

"Marriage and parenting are difficult enough, but throw in a spouse who doesn't agree with your faith—well, only God can redeem that situation, which is exactly the hope Nancy Sebastian Meyer offers in *Spiritually Single Moms*. Nancy's honesty and transparency and the tough lessons learned are gifts from Him to the rest of us."

—NANCY KENNEDY, author of *When He Doesn't Believe*

"With the voice of a caring and understanding friend, Nancy Sebastian Meyer combines personal experience with biblical truth to speak comfort, encouragement, and hope to the hearts of women. This treasure of a book is overflowing with wise counsel and practical help for the spiritually single mom."

—GINGER PLOWMAN, author of *Don't Make Me Count to Three* and *Heaven at Home*

"In practical, wise, gentle, and loving ways, Nancy Sebastian Meyer is living the life of a spiritually single mom raising a godly child. It can be done! And Meyer shows you how with strategies, Scripture, stories, and self-assessment. As encouragement in their sacred and enormous task, I plan to give this book to some spiritually single moms I know."

NIXON, MA, speaker; columnist; *Parenting Power in the Early Years*

Nancy Sebastian Meyer

Spiritually

Single

Moms

Raising Godly Kids When Dad Doesn't Believe

NAVPRESS®

BRINGING TRUTH TO LIFE

OUR GUARANTEE TO YOU

We believe so strongly in the message of our books that we are making this quality guarantee to you. If for any reason you are disappointed with the content of this book, return the title page to us with your name and address and we will refund to you the list price of the book. To help us serve you better, please briefly describe why you were disappointed. Mail your refund request to: NavPress, P.O. Box 35002, Colorado Springs, CO 80935.

The Navigators is an international Christian organization. Our mission is to advance the gospel of Jesus and His kingdom into the nations through spiritual generations of laborers living and discipling among the lost. We see a vital movement of the gospel, fueled by prevailing prayer, flowing freely through relational networks and out into the nations where workers for the kingdom are next door to everywhere.

NavPress is the publishing ministry of The Navigators. The mission of NavPress is to reach, disciple, and equip people to know Christ and make Him known by publishing life-related materials that are biblically rooted and culturally relevant. Our vision is to stimulate spiritual transformation through every product we publish.

ISBN-13: 978-1-57683-874-7
ISBN-10: 1-57683-874-9

Cover design by studiogearbox.com
Cover photo by Veer/Stockbyte
Creative Team: Terry Behimer, Liz Heaney, Reagen Reed, Kathy Mosier, Arvid Wallen, Kathy Guist

Some of the anecdotal illustrations in this book are true to life and are included with the permission of the persons involved. All other illustrations are composites of real situations, and any resemblance to people living or dead is coincidental.

Unless otherwise identified, all Scripture quotations in this publication are taken from the HOLY BIBLE: NEW INTERNATIONAL VERSION® (NIV®). Copyright © 1973, 1978, 1984 by International Bible Society. Used by permission of Zondervan Publishing House. All rights reserved. Other versions used include: *THE MESSAGE* (MSG). Copyright © 1993, 1994, 1995, 1996, 2000, 2001, 2002. Used by permission of NavPress Publishing Group; the *Amplified New Testament* (AMP), © The Lockman Foundation 1954, 1958; and the *King James Version* (KJV).

Meyer, Nancy Sebastian, 1961-
  Spiritually single moms : raising godly kids when dad doesn't believe
/ Nancy Sebastian Meyer.
    p. cm.
  Includes bibliographical references.
  ISBN 1-57683-874-9
  1. Parenting--Religious aspects--Christianity. 2. Child
rearing--Religious aspects--Christianity. 3. Mothers--Religious life.
4. Non-church-affiliated people--Family relationships. I. Title.
BV4529.18.M49 2006
248.8'431--dc22
                        2006024359

Printed in the United States of America

1 2 3 4 5 6 / 11 10 09 08 07

FOR A FREE CATALOG OF NAVPRESS BOOKS & BIBLE STUDIES,
CALL 1-800-366-7788 (USA) OR 1-800-839-4769 (CANADA).

Contents

Acknowledgments

Rich, my husband, thank you for being the very best dad for Becky, and thank you for giving me permission to share our story.

Becky, our loving daughter, may God keep your heart teachable and fill it with His truth and joy in all circumstances.

Karen Stoltzfus, my praying friend and proofreader, and Janelle, Laurie, Nancy, and other spiritually single moms, as well as additional friends who read the original manuscript, thank you for sharing suggestions and encouragement.

Faithful prayer partners, thank you for your unfailing, front-line efforts in prayer.

Liz Heaney, editor extraordinaire, thank you for partnering with me, for making me think and dig and rewrite, so this book can reflect God's truth with accuracy and excellence.

A Personal Note to Spiritually Single Moms

(From the Author's Daughter)

Dear "Mom,"

You are an extreme influence on your children. They see everything, even your mistakes. But just like God's forgiveness is boundless, so is theirs. I honor and respect my mom for the times she fails, asks for forgiveness, and tries again. I love her humble willingness to learn from her mistakes. She is a great example.

Your children need you in your spiritually divided home. They need to see God through your eyes. They need your teaching and encouragement. Unfortunately, as they enter their teen years, they will turn to peers for answers to their questions, even questions about God. The good news is that no matter how distant your teenagers seem to become, they will still look to you for much of their guidance and teaching. My mom has taught me most of the valuable lessons in life that I've learned. I know I've sometimes made it hard for her. We don't always see eye-to-eye, but eventually we talk about almost everything. And Mom is my biggest cheerleader.

Although my dad sometimes doesn't get where I'm coming from spiritually, Mom reminds me to extend God's grace and work on the sin in my own life. I love her so much for the heritage of godliness she has passed down to me. But as Mom would put it, "to God be the glory!"

Sincerely,
Becky Meyer

If you are a spiritually single parent, or you know someone who is, this book is for you. Bookstore shelves and grocery store magazine racks brim with self-help literature for parents. But I wrote this book for a special segment of the tired parent population — moms like me who have a spouse who is absent, apathetic, or antagonistic toward God. It contains hope and help for moms who desire to raise godly children — specifically those women whose jobs are made ever so much more difficult and uncertain because *Dad doesn't believe.*

Although each chapter can stand alone in its topic and truths, the book as a whole addresses the spectrum of challenges and needs you have as a spiritually single parent. At the end of each chapter you will find four sections.

Strength gives a key verse that confirms the focus of the chapter.

If You Are a Spiritually Single Dad. . .

While I wrote this book for spiritually single moms in situations similar to mine, God's truths are not gender-specific. You can apply the information to your situation, although you may have to adjust some of these concepts so they address a masculine perspective. Ask the Holy Spirit to accompany you on your journey through these truths. He is the ultimate Counselor and Guide, not only through this book, but on a much grander scale throughout life. He longs to walk with you.

Strategies offers bulleted points pertaining to the practical working out of the chapter's basic truths.

Self-Assessment provides a list of questions whose honest answers will lead you to a deeper, more obedient walk with God through these tough parenting years.

Speaking with God contains a prayer based on the acrostic P-R-A-Y (*Praise*, *Repent*, *Ask*, and *Yield*).

This book will speak to different hearts in different ways, because each reader and her circumstance is unique, yet *God's truth is appropriate and applicable in every situation.* By helping us put His Word into practice, God is able to work out His will in the life of every believer for His glory and our good. Pray, trust, read, and apply under the tutelage of the Holy Spirit, the divine Counselor.

I've found strength in these godly principles, and you can too. God desires to meet you this very moment and take you onward *from here.* It is never too late. Come with me and find rest for your weariness, simplicity to replace the stress in your life, and an ever-present Friend who will walk with you throughout the remainder of your life.

Dear heavenly Father,
you are the divine Parent.
We, your children, come to you weary, stressed, and lonely.
Life is not what we anticipated or desired—
but you are everything we need.
Thank you.
Please teach us, Holy Spirit, wisest of counselors.
In Jesus' name, and for His sake,
Amen.

Chapter 1

When Dad Doesn't Believe

I shifted my position in the pew, once again wishing that Rich, my husband, would fill the empty seat beside me. The worship team began leading congregational singing, but the words of praise and thanksgiving stuck in my throat. Later, when the choir sang "I trust you, Lord," tears burned the back of my eyelids and blurred my vision—not because I couldn't trust God, but because I could do nothing but trust Him. God, my solid rock through changing seasons, storms, and situations beyond my control.

My mind wandered back a few months to when Rich's faith had begun to waver. "My prayers are hitting the ceiling, Nancy. I can't see God or feel Him. I'm not even sure He's there," the Bible college graduate and former youth pastor admitted. "I'm not going to go to church with you and sit there like a hypocrite. I'm going to take a little break and think this out."

Fifteen years later, my husband concedes that God probably exists, but he believes that one cannot experience a personal relationship with Him. This incredibly intelligent man, with a will of iron and determination like granite, will not give over the control of his life to anyone or anything that he cannot understand and figure out. Rich is a faithful, loving husband and father, but in many respects he is a different person from the youth pastor I married twenty years ago. Although he allows me to share our story "so women will hang on in difficult marriages and not break up families," he's still sidelined on Sundays, and I go alone.

Initially, I tried my best to change Rich. I attempted to be a perfect person, pushing myself almost to the point of a breakdown, believing I needed to save my marriage and spouse. I tried so hard to be everything to everyone else's satisfaction that I couldn't even fulfill tasks in my areas of strength. All my efforts to "fix" my husband didn't work.

And I felt so alone.

I felt alone when I buckled my daughter into her car seat and headed for church without my husband. I felt alone when I read a bedtime Bible story to her without her dad. I felt alone when I helped Becky practice a memory verse or say her prayers while Rich was downstairs reading.

But I have never felt more alone than the day seven-year-old Becky said, "Mom, I've got something to tell you that I don't know if I should say." I held my breath, wondering what was coming. "Mom, half my heart believes in Jesus, but the other half doesn't know if He's real. What am I gonna do?"

Her earnest question grieved my already aching heart. I knew Becky would notice her dad's and my spiritual differences someday, but I still felt unprepared for her question. My mind immediately filled with angry thoughts about Rich: *If only you had held fast to your beliefs, Becky wouldn't be wrestling with this insecurity!* Next, I started in on God: *You knew before we married that our lives would turn out like this. You could have stopped us. You could have saved Becky.*

Then I remembered whom I was addressing and confessed, *I am wrong to blame you. You do know everything, and right now I need to know what you want me to say to my child!*

Extracting the first coherent thought from my Bible college–trained brain, I said, "Honey, God doesn't mind when we question Him and doubt—because He knows we're human. He just wants us to ask Him about it."

As I led the way into her bedroom, I continued, "Let's find the part in your Bible about doubting Thomas. Do you remember studying him in Sunday school?" I pulled Becky's Bible off the shelf as we sat together on the bed. I couldn't get my fingers to find the story of Thomas in the Gospels, and we "somehow" ended up in Jeremiah. I began to read a few underlined verses: "'For I know the plans I have for you,' declares the LORD, 'plans to prosper you and not to harm you, plans to give you hope and a future'" (29:11). As we continued to read, I realized that I was not alone. Never had been. Never would be.

God's transforming power in my life over the past twelve years worked changes in me that have turned me into the wife and mother I am today, the wife and mother God calls and equips me to be. The changes in me, in turn, have brought love, hope, and peace back to our family, even in the midst of my husband's lack of faith. Perhaps most incredible, miraculous even, is Rich's permission for me to write and speak about our story.

You Are Never Alone

Dear friend, can you relate? Have you ever asked yourself if you married the wrong man? Have you ever wondered when your husband will get serious about his relationship with God? Do you long for your husband to assume his God-ordained position as spiritual leader of your home?

If you answered "yes" to any of these questions, you belong to a large contingency of women. Even women married to church officials and pastors often harbor secret desires for greater spiritual intimacy with their spouse.

Whether or not you recognize God or feel His gentle touch in your life, He is with you. You are not alone. He's been a part of your life and in step with you since you became His precious child. And He will never leave you. Check for yourself in Hebrews 13:5:

> *"Never will I leave you;*
> *never will I forsake you."*

To spiritually single moms, God says:

> *"Come to me, all you who are weary and burdened,*
> *and I will give you rest. Take my yoke upon you and*
> *learn from me, for I am gentle and humble in heart,*
> *and you will find rest for your souls. For my yoke is*
> *easy and my burden is light."*
>
> Matthew 11:28-30

> *"Surely I am with you always, to the very end of the age."*
> 28:20

We may be spiritually single, but we're never alone.

Practice His Presence

Don't just agree with me — experience it for yourself. Look for Him in the little things that happen during your day. Listen for

Him in the singing of the birds and the splash of a waterfall. Breathe deeply, close your eyes, and find Him in the stillness of a quiet moment. Hear Him in the laughter of children. Feel Him in the hug of a dear friend. See Him in tonight's sunset. Talk to Him throughout your day whenever you need someone with whom to share a pleasant thought or a troubling problem. Go to bed with Him as you praise Him for the blessings of the day.

Teach your children that God is with us in every situation. For example, when a difficult circumstance arises in your husband's life and his angry response or behavior upsets your children, sit down alone with them and explain just as much as they need to know. Then pray together for Dad and his situation. Or while doing a chore with a child, bring God naturally into the conversation by asking your child how he or she has seen God today—and let that lead into thanking God for what He's doing in your family.

Practice His presence day after day after day.

Guard Your Heart

About two years after Rich stopped going to church with me, I returned to my home church where my parents still worshipped. I needed family. My tattered heart began to heal as week after week my precious mom and dad sat me right between them in the pew.

Many good friends attended a Sunday school class for couples. Because I was diligently praying for Rich's spiritual restoration, I joined the class with the hope that Rich would soon be attending, too. Unfortunately, that never happened. Instead, every week I sat with girlfriends and their husbands—the yucky boys I grew up with in junior church who had matured into tall, handsome, godly men. I had rejoined a church filled with tempting examples of godly manhood everywhere I looked. Yikes!

A few months later, I sat in the car in our garage with Rich after we'd come home from an evening out. With that heightened awareness that comes during a moment of crisis, I admitted to him I was scared that I would fall for some godly, kind man at church—not because of anything inappropriate on the other person's part, but because my heart was vulnerable. Good man that he is, Rich sat with me in silence for a few minutes and then asked what he could do to help me. Just telling him about my need—and it was difficult—helped me face the temptation. I resolved in my heart to flee it and run back to my first love, my husband.

At church, in other ordinary places, or even on the Internet, a spiritually single mom can find herself becoming attracted to a kind man who seems to be everything spiritually that her husband is not. But if she loses her heart to someone else—even if she never touches him—she will further damage her relationship with her husband and possibly harm her reputation with her children (if they are old enough to understand the situation).

How can you protect your heart when it seems so vulnerable?

1. Acknowledge the possible problem.
2. Flee temptation. (I had to give up singing in the choir to avoid a man who touched my heart with his kind, gentle ways *with other people—not even me!*)
3. Confess your fears and vulnerable heart to a friend who will help hold you accountable.

4. Focus your love and attention where it belongs — on your husband. (You will find help for this last point in my book for wives, *Beyond Expectations: Finding Joy In Your Marriage*. Yes, you can fall in love with your husband all over again — even if your love tank seems to be on empty right now.)

But it's not only our hearts that are vulnerable. So is our total well-being, and our ability to be the women, wives, and moms we need to be.

Keep in Balance

A juggler at an amusement park caught my interest by spinning a plate atop a long pole. As the plate kept spinning, he called a teenager over and handed the boy the pole. The juggler continued launching plates and handing them to people. Every so often a plate began to wobble, and with one finger he would nonchalantly send it back into smooth orbit.

Finally, he chose a participant from the audience, handed her a plate and pole, and motioned for her to launch the spinning plate. She tried, without success. Before the young woman gave up in frustration, he leaned over and guided her hands through the correct motions. The plate began to spin, and the crowd clapped wildly.

One by one, participants were asked to relinquish their plates and poles back to the juggler. He made the first few props disappear with a flourish behind the curtain, while encouraging us to applaud his helpers. Then we watched with astonishment as he retrieved and began balancing the remaining five — one on his head, one on a foot, another on the knee of the same leg, one in his right hand, and the last in his left hand. He kept them all spinning with slight jerks on the corresponding body part. The crowd enthusiastically applauded its approval and respect.

Every mom, like this juggler, must keep many tasks and obligations spinning within her control. In God's perfect plan, her husband helps her. Together they balance each other and their family responsibilities. This picture breaks down for the single or divorced mom, who is solely in charge of every aspect of her family. Likewise, the spiritually single mom often feels unsupported and unbalanced as she seeks to carry the spiritual load of the family on her shoulders.

All of us feel overwhelmed from time to time. It seems Satan often selects moments such as these to top off our problems with spiritual dissention in the house. How can you cope? What can you do to safeguard against falling apart at times like this? If God could resurrect His own Son, He has the power to provide you with everything you need for doing His will and can work in you what is pleasing to Him (see Hebrews 13:20-21).

Let's take a moment to break down the areas of our lives and to look at what God has to say about our personal balancing act. After all, He created us as multifaceted people — and what He created He called "good"!

Every person has these five interrelated parts: spiritual, mental, emotional, social, and physical. The writer of Hebrews addressed all five of these aspects:

> Let us draw near to God with a sincere heart in
> full assurance of faith [spiritual], having our hearts
> sprinkled to cleanse us from a guilty conscience
> [mental] and having our bodies washed with pure
> water [physical]. Let us hold unswervingly to the

*hope [emotional] we profess, for he who promised is
faithful. And let us consider how we may spur one
another on toward love and good deeds. Let us not
give up meeting together [social].*

10:22-25

It's important for spiritually single moms to attend to all
five of these areas and to keep them in balance, so let's take a
look at how you can do that. As you read, give yourself a check-
up. How are you doing and where do you need to improve?

- Satisfy your *spirit* with the Water of Life by reading God's
  Word every day and spending time thinking about Him
  and talking to Him about your joys and concerns (see John
  7:37-38).
- Transform your *thoughts* from the world's standards
  to God's principles by memorizing and meditating on
  Scripture and by testing everything against the truth in
  God's Word. As Scripture tells us, "Test everything. Hold
  on to the good. Avoid every kind of evil" (1 Thessalonians
  5:21-22).
- Rejoice in the Lord always and think about the good and
  positive things in your life (see Philippians 4:4,8), which
  will produce the healthy *emotions* of joy and peace.
- Meet together in church and elsewhere with fellow believers who can offer you two types of *social* encouragement:
  comfort and accountability (see Hebrews 10:25).
- Practice healthy eating, sleeping, and exercise routines to
  keep energized for the Lord's work and present a healthy
  physical being—the temple of the Holy Spirit (see 1
  Corinthians 6:19-20).

Indeed, all the parts of us are "fearfully and wonderfully made" (Psalm 139:14). But when one part starts wobbling, all of the other parts are at risk. So pay attention to your own needs. If your life is not in balance, you won't be much help to those around you, especially the ones you most need to influence—your children.

Just as the juggler learned and practiced spinning his plates, we moms must learn and practice keeping our lives balanced. We need peace within before we can expect to get our outward act together. But God's Word promises:

> *Those who hope in the Lord*
> *will renew their strength.*
> *They will soar on wings like eagles;*
> *they will run and not grow weary,*
> *they will walk and not be faint.*

Isaiah 40:31

Our Lord is ready and willing to help you. Will you let Him?

Strength

> *"Never will I leave you;*
> *never will I forsake you."*

Hebrews 13:5

Strategies

- Many Christian moms feel alone in raising children to love God.
- We need to recognize that we can't change anyone but ourselves. Only God can enliven a person's heart toward Him.

- God is in the midst of the tiniest details of our lives. He will never leave us or forsake us.
- We must practice God's presence in our lives, exercising all five senses and our faith.
- A crucial priority is guarding our hearts from emotional temptations.
- God perfectly created each human being with five inter-related facets — spiritual, mental, emotional, social, and physical.
- Balancing these five areas is a learned skill, which requires regular practice for the entirety of life.

Self-Assessment

1. Ask God to reveal any feelings of loneliness and anger within you (see Psalm 139:23). Then write down your thoughts and feelings, and sort them out with God. (This often helps me process thoughts so I can understand God more clearly.)

2. Can you remember a place and time when you accepted God's gift of forgiveness, love, and belonging? Do you know you are His child? If not, will you pray and tell Him you accept the fact you are a sinner and believe that Jesus died for your sins? You can become His child forever (see 2 Corinthians 5:14-21). Ask Him, today, to take away your old nature and make you a new person in Him.

3. When was the last time you experienced God's presence? What happened? (See page 63 for how to spend a whole day looking for evidence of God.)

4. Do you believe there is nothing you can do that will make God love you more, and there is nothing you can ever do that will make Him love you less than He does at this very moment? Why or why not?

5. What are you doing to protect your heart?

Speaking with God

Dear heavenly Father,
I praise you for your continued presence by my side
as you offer to help me balance my responsibilities.
I repent of not always being on the same page with you
in all the aspects of my life.
Please give me more faith and wisdom to live
according to your divine direction.
I yield myself to your plan for my life today.

Chapter 2

Keeping Your Focus on God

A normal day in the life of a mother contains any number of situations—expected and unexpected—that require split-second decisions, calculations, and judgments. How we think about those things determines our attitude and response.

"Mom, I have to have that shirt *now*! I thought you said you were gonna do the laundry yesterday."

Oops! I did say that, didn't I? But so many other urgent things came up yesterday. I can't do it all!

"Hon, you're a stay-at-home mom. Why can't you manage simple errands I ask you to run for me?"

I can't believe I forgot to pick up his dry cleaning . . . again! I know he thinks I don't do anything all day while he's hard at work.

"That's not fair, Ma. You didn't ground Jeremy when he did that!"

Am I being too hard on him? No. Maybe. I don't know!

"Why can't I have Allison come for a sleepover this weekend? You're so mean!"

I want to have a great mom-daughter relationship with her, so should I say "yes"?

"Katie just called and needs to be picked up at school. Did you forget or are you just late . . . again?"

Just because you're always early doesn't mean I'm going to forget our daughter at softball. You could go pick her up yourself! Oh, gosh, that didn't sound very godly.

Can you relate? If so, how can we keep focused on God and respond appropriately when life feels overwhelming?

Have the Mind of Christ

First, we must realize the importance of our thoughts. Yes, the initial problem may be an outside attack (a husband's criticism or child's complaint), but we possess control over how we process unkind or disrespectful words and how we will react.

Paul told the Corinthians, "We have the mind of Christ" (1 Corinthians 2:16). Then he later explained to the Colosse church, "Since, then, you have been raised with Christ, set your hearts on things above, where Christ is seated at the right hand of God. Set your minds on things above, not on earthly things. For you died, and your life is now hidden with Christ in God" (Colossians 3:1-3).

Paul is encouraging us to have the mind of Christ because he knows that what we think about—our thoughts, beliefs, and convictions—becomes what we feel and do. Our thoughts initiate a chain reaction. If we focus on our fears, frustrations, or disappointments, it's going to affect our behavior and attitude, including how we treat our children and spouse. Here's an illustration of how this works:

Let's say your eight-year-old daughter knocks over a glass of milk at breakfast. This isn't the first time something like this has happened, and thoughts like these fill your mind: *I can't believe she's so clumsy! Now I'm going to be late to work because I have to clean up this mess before I take her to school.* You snap at your daughter, saying, "How many times do I have to tell you to be more careful? I don't know what I'm going to do with you, young lady! Brush your teeth and go wait for me in the car—I don't want you to make me any more late for work than you already have!" She leaves the table in tears, and you think, *She's just a kid—why did I have to be so hard on her? After all, it wasn't like she spilled the milk on purpose . . . what kind of a mother am I?* How do you feel? Angry, upset, and guilty.

Yet, Paul says we have the mind of Christ. How can you apply Colossians 3:1-3 to this scenario?

First, recognize that the guilt you feel is from the Holy Spirit, who is convicting you of sin. Then, confess your angry response to God. Next, confess to your daughter your inappropriate reaction. Sincerely ask her forgiveness in order to restore your relationship.

Having the mind of Christ means being sensitive to the Holy Spirit's conviction and then taking the necessary steps to make our hearts right with God and with the person we have wronged. When we live this way, we are living "in Christ." We are also modeling righteous living.

Another way in which we can ensure that we keep a godly focus is by remembering that we are engaged in a spiritual battle.

Always Remember Who Your Real Enemy Is

As spiritually single moms we can never forget this truth:

> *For though we live in the world, we do not wage war*
> *as the world does. The weapons we fight with are not*

*the weapons of the world. On the contrary, they have
divine power to demolish strongholds. We demolish
arguments and every pretension that sets itself up
against the knowledge of God, and we take captive
every thought to make it obedient to Christ.*

2 Corinthians 10:3-5

Make no mistake about it—a vicious but often subtle war exists in our homes. Spiritual warfare rages in the life of every Christian. It can be easy for us spiritually single moms to tell ourselves that if our husbands were united with us spiritually, then we wouldn't have such battles and our lives would be easier because we would "ride shotgun" for each other. This perspective, which is wrong, causes us to feel like the odd man out, making our fight that much tougher—and lonelier.

That's why it's so important for us to remind ourselves of this truth: *My husband is not the opponent.* Satan is!

One of the primary ways you as a spiritually single mom can have the "mind of Christ" is to remember that you and your husband are members of the same team (even if you sometimes play by different rules). Such a perspective allows you to sustain a gracious attitude toward your spouse, as you:

- head off to Bible study alone
- pray with your daughter regarding an important decision in her life
- talk with your son about God's view of sex
- confront your teenager's resistance to going to church every Sunday

So, the next time you feel alone in your efforts to raise godly children, rather than resent your husband or feel sorry for yourself, remember you have a supernatural ally in the Holy Spirit, who is always present, all-powerful, and tuned in to the enemy's next move. First Thessalonians 5:24 says, "The one who calls you is faithful and he will do it." With your call to be a wife and mother, God promises to equip you, enable you, and fight right alongside you.

Even if your home is a pleasant, peaceful place to live day to day, know that spiritual warfare is going on behind the scenes in each family member's life. Each of us is constantly engaged in the battle between right and wrong. We moms must be ready at a second's notice to defeat evil with truth.

We can do this by implementing some simple, but profound steps that keep us "at the ready."

Keep "At the Ready"

Spring-clean your mind. Have you ever considered how nice your house feels after you've done some major cleaning? The air is fresh, the table tops shine, and the appliances sparkle. Cleaning our minds takes place when we confess sins by identifying wrongs we've committed against God and agreeing with Him that they are sins—"calling a spade a spade."

Be ruthless in your clean-up efforts:

> *You were taught, with regard to your former way of life, to put off your old self, which is being corrupted by its deceitful desires; to be made new in the attitude of your minds; and to put on the new self, created to be like God in true righteousness and holiness.*
>
> Ephesians 4:22-24

The rest of Ephesians 4 sheds light on what to remove from

your life: anger, bitterness, rage, and unforgiveness. But don't stop there.

What earthly thoughts, desires, or vices are you entertaining? Addictions come in every color, shape, and size — many of which seem so innocent. The words *fixation*, *inclination*, *bent*, and *habit* are all more or less synonyms for "addiction." When anything but God is our chief focus, we dilute His strength and power in our lives. As spiritually single moms, we need more of His strength, not less!

Addictions can be very subtle. This was brought home to me several years ago when I began playing a computer game designed for kids. The more I won, the more I wanted to play. Eventually I realized that playing this game had become my primary focus. I wasted hours playing this game, hours I couldn't afford! The game was not the problem; the problem was that I had allowed it to become too great a desire and priority. When I realized what I was doing, I repented, gave the game to my husband for safe-keeping, and chose not to play it at all for well over a year. Now, on the rare occasion I play that game, I turn it off the first time I lose rather than playing again and again in succession.

What entanglements do you need to remove from your life by God's grace? Get rid of them!

But even when we are trying to keep clean before God, we don't always recognize the sin in our lives. Sin hides itself from us. That's why, every once in a while, I will kneel at my quiet time chair, confess all the sin I know about, and ask God to show me anything else that is wrong in my life. Then I wait. In the quietness, I mentally replay the last day or two — even events within the past week or so — and allow God to focus my attention. Inevitably, I see a sin that was previously hidden from me, and confess it. Then I wait again, see another sin, and confess it. I continue to wait, see, and confess until I feel squeaky clean before the Holy Spirit. Try this for yourself.

Better yet, keep short accounts with God by confessing sin as soon as it happens or when you become aware of it. Intentionally keep your mind clean and pure by maintaining a guard on what goes in your eyes and ears. Deliberately spend time in God's Word so you can renew your thinking, as Paul recommended in Romans 12:2: "Do not conform any longer to the pattern of this world, but be transformed by the renewing of your mind. Then you will be able to test and approve what God's will is—his good, pleasing and perfect will."

Polish the sword of God's Word. Memorizing and hiding God's Word in your heart gives the Holy Spirit something to bring to your mind when you need God's Word of encouragement, truth, or instruction in a given situation. If it's not there, He can't help you remember it. Tell yourself the truth—God's truth!

Ask God to show you key verses that will help you in difficult circumstances. Then begin an active program of memorization. Make it simple, but keep the verses you are memorizing in handy places where you can work on them in spare moments (in your wallet to review in the grocery line, in your car to practice at red lights . . .). Review previous verses often to keep them fresh. It helps to partner with a friend who is also memorizing; you can hold each other accountable. If you are not sure where to begin, start with some of the verses you find in this book.

I know firsthand the truth of this verse: "The Word of God is living and active. Sharper than any double-edged sword, it penetrates even to dividing soul and spirit, joints and marrow; it judges the thoughts and attitudes of the heart" (Hebrews 4:12). When a phrase from a verse pops up in my conscious thoughts and I recognize it as God's Word, I concentrate on repeating the words again and again, thinking about them, analyzing how they pertain to the situation at hand.

Just a few nights ago, my mind was racing with concerns and coming responsibilities that threatened to overwhelm me. I deliberately started quoting the first few words of Philippians 4:6, which say, "Do not be anxious about anything." As I rehearsed this instruction in my mind, I willed myself to turn my worries over to God's strong shoulders so I could sleep. Sleep wasn't instantaneous, but little by little my mind slowed and my body relaxed so I could rest.

In another instance, God prompted me to confront Rich about a situation, and as I anticipated our conversation, Ephesians 4:15 replayed continuously in my mind: "Speaking the truth in love, we will in all things grow up into him who is the Head, that is, Christ." This verse gave me the courage I needed to say hard words to even harder ears—but God had compassion on me and gave me favor in Rich's sight that day.

God's words can replace my fears with confidence, give me compassion for others involved in the situation, and clarify the details. This is the outworking of 2 Timothy 1:7, which says, "For God did not give us a spirit of timidity [also translated "fear," KJV], but a spirit of power, of love and of self-discipline ["a sound mind," KJV]."

However, please beware of using God's Word to batter your unbelieving husband with truths you think he needs to recognize. Only God convicts and opens the heart to His truth. While you should certainly live out biblical truth in front of your spouse, the spoken word may fall on deaf ears. Constant attempts to verbalize your faith and understanding of God's Word may make the situation worse. If your husband asks or the situation is appropriate and you feel the nudge of the Holy Spirit, by all means open your mouth and speak. Then let God's Spirit take those brief, truthful words and apply them to the man's heart. Trust God and go on your way, walking in the truth.

Think with the Holy Spirit. This point relates directly to the last one. The Holy Spirit, who lives within you from the moment you accept Jesus as Savior, wants to have a personal relationship with you. He desires to be your best friend—with you all the time, whispering just what to do in each situation, laughing with you over something funny or delightful, and commiserating when life stinks.

Remembering that the Spirit is with us takes practice. It is easy to forget. He is invisible. But we spiritually single moms need His active presence in our lives. We need to interact with Him by asking Him questions, rehearsing ideas and thoughts, and thanking Him for things.

For example, during those times when I'm in a difficult situation with Rich or Becky, I often ask God, "Should I say something now or remain quiet? Is it my place to step in or are you going to take care of this another way? Who needs to be ministered to right now? How can I help?" This pattern of thinking keeps me focused on God's will about the situation, instead of growing negative as I contemplate what and who is wrong. Over time, this exercise can become as natural as breathing. And I am modeling for my daughter how to learn to listen to God's truth.

When I'm focused on Him, the Holy Spirit never fails to prompt me to say and do the right thing in a situation. His response to me is always in line with Scripture. I know a thought is *not* from Him if I can't prove it based on the Bible or on the character of God. (If I can't think of or find a verse to prove something, I line it up against what I know of God's character. If it doesn't measure up, I know it is not from Him.)

As I practice "thinking with the Holy Spirit," I also obey what the Bible has already told me about how God thinks. Philippians 4:8 tells me to think about things that are true, noble, right, pure, lovely, admirable, excellent, and praiseworthy. Philippians 2:3 instructs me to consider others and look to their interests. I want to keep my mind focused on what God's best is in each situation, not on what I want or what I think is best. I am training my mind to think about truth, others, and the positive aspects of everything.

God has the ability to read your mind, so you may as well voluntarily share your thoughts with Him. Throughout your day—when you wash the dishes, do the laundry, drive to the grocery store or to pick up your kids—acknowledge that the Spirit is with you and allow Him to direct your thoughts or help you think through something that is troubling you.

If you put these three things into practice, you will gain strength, guidance, and direction as you seek to raise godly children, even though your spouse isn't your partner in this endeavor. As you practice these truths, you are teaching your children to do the same—you are practicing what you preach.

In addition to "keeping at the ready," I have discovered a proactive way of keeping my mental focus on God and His will for my life—both for the short-term and for the long-term.

Maintain Godly Priorities

Every morning I ask God to reveal His truth about what *should* be most important to me that day. This helps me stay focused on God for the short-term. I've come to realize that life consists of many seasons. Just because something I want to do is good and godly, it does not mean it fits into God's plan for me *right now*.

I keep God in my long-term focus by writing out my mission statement at the beginning of each calendar year. Then I write down seven to ten basic goals (in the following priority order: God, husband, child, home, self, world, and miscellaneous) and a key verse(s) for the year. For example, here is what I wrote last year:

Mission Statement:

May I grow deeper in God this year so I might see with eyes like His, hear with ears like His, speak words consistent with His Word, and reach out with His love.

Goals:

1. I will daily read and meditate on God's Word. (God)
2. I will pray specifically once a day, lift up short prayers throughout each day, and partner in prayer with others. (God)
3. I will unconditionally love Rich, learn to listen to him, and speak the truth in love. (husband)
4. I will love Becky, school her wisely, and be a wise encourager. (child)
5. I will maintain household duties and a home environment that draws my family together. (home)
6. I will regularly exercise, drink water, and eat wisely to get to a healthy weight. (self)
7. I will get adequate rest, recharge/relax weekly, and attend my Sunday school class regularly. (self)
8. I will obey the Lord by using my gifts and talents to the best of my ability and all for His glory. (world)
9. I will keep my lifestyle pure and my conversation honoring to God. (world)
10. I will daily strive to be clean, available, learning, and leaning on Him. (miscellaneous)

Key Scripture:

> *Do not neglect your gift . . . be diligent . . . so that*
> *everyone may see your progress. Watch your life and*
> *doctrine closely. Persevere in them, because if you do,*
> *you will save both yourself and your hearers.*
>
> 1 Timothy 4:14-16

My mission statement and goals don't change much from year to year, but the activity of writing them out helps me remain focused on God and the priorities I believe He has given me.

I print my goals on a half-sheet of paper and put one copy above my desk and another in the front of my Bible. Often on Sunday mornings before the worship service begins, I open my Bible and glance down through my goals—comparing them against my thoughts, actions, and schedule during the past week. This exercise helps keep me focused and balanced. Instead of waltzing through life, reacting to one problem after another, I'm living proactively. I get ahead of the problems before they overwhelm me.

In fact, just last week I glanced down at my goals and "get adequate rest" jumped out at me. I squirmed under the Holy Spirit's conviction as I remembered how late I'd gone to bed almost every night the previous week. Then I thought about how grouchy and unloving—selfish—I'd been with Rich and Becky throughout the week. I immediately confessed my lack of self-care and asked God to help me see ways to get more rest and to respond in a kinder, more godly way to my family in the upcoming week.

It's been said, "Aim at nothing, and you'll hit it every time." Articulated priorities can help us focus our energy on matters of importance and minimize detours that sap our time, energy, and resources. Priorities serve as anchors in the storms of life. They give us something to hang on to, something that can help us measure our lives and chart our progress. Are you regularly checking your life against your priorities and keeping your focus clear?

Below is a journal entry I wrote a few years ago after returning to my routines following a short period of having abandoned them. After the third week of disciplined, prioritized living—starting every day with God—I wrote:

> I experienced such joy this week. I think it came from the freedom of not worrying about what I was missing and what I was forgetting. Starting the week knowing my priorities and going over my schedule for the day with God first thing every morning gave me *confidence, boldness, and such incredible freedom.* And beyond these feelings, I accomplished so much! Why did I let this habit lapse?

I encourage you to create your own list of goals and priorities. As you do, be sure to consider all five aspects of your being, which we looked at in chapter 1—social, mental, emotional, physical, and spiritual. *Your highest priority should be your spiritual health, so be sure to schedule time with God and to treat spiritual fatigue.* If you need further help in the area of setting priorities, I recommend chapter 4 of Linda Dillow's book *Creative Counterpart*, called "The Priority Planner."

Stay Focused

Max Lucado's book *You Are Special,* written for children, speaks powerfully to adults about our daily need to focus on our Creator. In the story, a little wooden boy becomes distressed by other wooden people's insults, which he begins to believe are true. When he finally finds his way to the Woodcarver's shop, the Maker tells him not to listen to their lies. To the wooden boy's astonishment, the Maker tells him he is very special and He loves him very much. This is more than the boy can comprehend. But at the end of the story the Maker assures the boy he will understand, "but it will take time. For now, come to see me every day and let me remind you how much I care."[1]

While the story is about how special we are to God, I think it also illustrates another important truth: We need to visit God every day in order to remember who we are and to keep our focus on Him. So make it a priority to spend time with God—you won't *find* time; you must *make* time. Talk to Him about everything. Talk about Him with your children. Share both special moments and trying times with the Holy Spirit, your God-given Helper, on this truth-finding mission. John 16:13 tells us, "When he, the Spirit of truth, comes, he will guide you into all truth." Revel in the relationship God wants to enjoy with you! For "then you will know the truth, and the truth will set you free" (John 8:32).

Strength

> *Do not conform any longer to the pattern of this world, but be transformed by the renewing of your mind. Then you will be able to test and approve*

what God's will is — his good, pleasing and
perfect will.

Romans 12:2

Strategies

- Keep your mind fixed on God's truth.
- Maintain a gracious attitude toward your spouse by thinking: *We're on the same team, fighting against evil — not each other.*
- Clean your mind by confessing sin and identifying wrongs you've committed against God. Agree with Him that they are sin.
- Keep short accounts with God by confessing sin immediately.
- Think with the Spirit — acknowledge His presence with you and pay attention to His still, small voice of encouragement and instruction.
- Identifying priorities helps you keep on track by focusing your energy on matters of importance and minimizing unnecessary detours that sap your time, energy, and resources.
- Visit with God every day so that your thoughts will be clean and godly.

Self-Assessment

1. What areas of your thought life are impure? Check your life for sexual impurities via the Internet, inappropriate romance novels, or media — television and magazines.

2. What bitterness, hurt, or anger lingers in your mind from past situations? Can you release your spirit of unforgiveness and trust God to deal with the person or problem?

3. What lost or shattered expectations still have a grip on you? Can you release these to God and ask Him to help you go on from here?

4. What sins must you confess and turn over to Him? State sin as sin; God already sees and knows—He wants you to agree with Him.

5. What can you do to deliberately "set your mind on things above" every day?

6. Have you ever considered writing out a mission statement and setting priority-based goals for your life? What would be the benefits? How can you fit this into your schedule and who might help you and hold you accountable to do this?

7. In what ways can you guard your mind?

Speaking with God

Dear All-Knowing One,
I praise you for the gift of my mind and the ability to think
clearly about many things.
I repent of sinful, worldly, and impure thoughts.
Please reveal yourself to me and help me connect internally
with your Spirit,
resulting in clean, effective, and God-honoring thinking.
I yield myself to an ongoing relationship with you
as I focus my thoughts on you.

Chapter 3

Loving and Respecting Your Spouse

I had just finished teaching the fourth lesson in a Bible study class for wives when a young woman approached me, shaking her head. "I'm sorry, but I'm really not able to do the assignment this week. There's too much *wrong* in my husband's life to even begin complimenting him. And the fact he doesn't love the Lord makes him callused and cynical. I just don't think this exercise is worth the effort in my particular case."

Not one to be daunted in the face of truth, I finally convinced her to faithfully practice God's command to encourage her husband. She agreed to give him at least one verbal compliment every day for seven days.

The following week, she arrived at our classroom early. "You will never guess what happened!" she gushed, going on to tell me that by the end of the week her husband was smiling, joking with her and the kids, and had even taken the family out for ice cream. "I never would have believed it if I hadn't experienced it for myself. Compliments work!"

But husbands who rarely, if ever, receive compliments and praise do not always readily accept our kind words, and other women in the class had less exciting results. Their husbands voiced suspicion, wanting to know what their wives wanted — thinking they might be "buttering them up" for selfish gain. It took several more weeks for these wives to win over their husbands with sincere words of praise, encouragement, and respect.

God created men to need respect, recognition, and admiration, and His Word teaches us that praise, positive comments, and compliments lift up and encourage. However, many wives who accept their husbands also take them for granted. They do not actively compliment, praise, or verbally respect their husbands. So, even if you believe your husband is a good guy, you may have problems getting the words past your lips.

Some spiritually single moms withhold words of affirmation and stifle attitudes of gratitude toward their husband because, in the big picture, they don't think he's good enough to deserve praise. Others have already tried praising their husbands and received a discouraging response.

Regardless of where your husband is coming from and what he is thinking and believing, you are called by God to live with this man and love him and to influence your children for the Lord. Do you recognize and highly esteem your husband's God-given strengths? Do you gratefully recognize him as your God-designed counterpart — even if he doesn't? In this chapter we are going to take a closer look at how you can better love and respect your husband.

But first I want to give you some information that might help you understand why your husband may be resistant to spiritual things, particularly church attendance.

Understanding Why He May Hate Going to Church

Church should be a wonderful place where people—men and women—authentically worship God, receive teaching from God's Word, fellowship together, and serve the Lord in their community and around the world. Unfortunately, many churches today are having problems attracting men to lead, participate in, and even attend their services. The problem is of such magnitude that David Murrow wrote a book entitled *Why Men Hate Going to Church*.

In it he insightfully points out that church is a great place for women. We enjoy getting dressed up. We love to socialize, sing, pray about our needs, and listen to a sermon. We feel good about our time at church, even though we haven't accomplished anything of magnitude. Men, however, sometimes perceive church as a place for women, but not for men. After all, what red-blooded, able-bodied man wants to sing songs, spill his guts, and listen to stories?

Murrow encourages spiritually single wives to try thinking about their church from their husband's perspective. What is there for a man to *do* in the church? A church can only have so many leaders, so most men who attend church simply sit, listen, and then go home. The problem is, males are created with testosterone—they are wired to accomplish. They need something to do, something to fight, something to win. So we put them on a committee (which some define as "a group of the unwilling, chosen from the unfit, to do the unnecessary"). Murrow points out that "men are achievement oriented and have little tolerance for a team that always plays defense and never plays offense."[2] Could this be a key to your husband's resistance to church? Is your church simply defending the faith, or is it advancing the gospel locally and abroad with vision and godly enthusiasm?

Of course, it may be that your husband, like mine, used to be very involved in church and then became disillusioned. When we were first married, Rich appeared to have a sincere faith and, as a youth pastor, was very involved in church and ministry. While I cannot know his heart and motives, I wonder if he was doing these things *for* God, instead of doing them *with* God. Ephesians 2:10 says, "For we are God's workmanship, created in Christ Jesus to do good works, which God prepared in advance for us to do." Working *for* Christ is part of being a Christian, but the things we do come directly out of our *relationship with* God, and we do them *with* God.

When we do things *for* God, we can easily get caught in the performance trap. We hope God likes what we do and that He blesses it . . . and if He doesn't we feel cheated. What we must realize is life is not about us and our plans. God's plans are the only thing that matters. He wants to do everything we do *with* us (see Jeremiah 29:11).

The essence of Christianity is simply being God's friend. Trust and obey Him, walk with Him, spend every moment of your day side-by-side with Him. It seems to me that it's easier for women to be dependent upon God than it is for men. Our culture, as well as the inner wiring of a man, demands he be the leader—strong, proud, and invincible. But Christ says, "Take my yoke upon you and learn from me, for I am gentle and humble in heart, and you will find rest for your souls" (Matthew 11:29).

If your husband claims to be a believer who is just turned-off to church, I encourage you to read Murrow's book. In it he says,

Women attend church in greater numbers than men. This is true all over the world, in nearly every

branch of Christianity. . . . Women are more serious about their faith. They are much more likely than men to participate in the life of the church beyond Sunday morning worship services. They are also more likely to practice Christian disciplines such as prayer, discipleship, and evangelism.[3]

Do not allow these words to make you feel smug. Murrow goes on to suggest that we women need to do some rethinking when it comes to trying to reach out to our men who don't like church. Here is a summary of what he encourages us to do to bring men back into the church. As you read through this list, ask God to show you which point(s) you need to emphasize in your relationship with your husband.

- Be willing to let your husband choose a church that meets his needs.
- Allow him to gather with other men, without any women around.
- Meet with other women to pray for your husbands.
- Stop dragging your husband to church with you—Jesus never forced anyone to follow Him.
- Be more real and less saintly and religious.
- Do not serve in a ministry to which God does not call you—you may be taking the place God has assigned to a man.
- Seek to be humble and compassionate, rather than demonstrating attitudes that belittle or come across as spiritually superior.
- Don't hold back from following Jesus with your whole heart.

- Give up your fantasy of what your husband will be like when God gets a hold of him, and start genuinely loving him and appreciating his strengths now.[4]

By paying attention to these things, you can minimize real or perceived condemnation toward your husband and encourage him to personally pursue a quest for truth . . . and God. Read back through the items on this list. Notice how they demonstrate an attitude of respect for your husband.

Respecting Him, Despite Your Differences

What is respect? Ephesians 5:33 says, "Let the wife see that she respects and reverences her husband—that she notices him, regards him, honors him, prefers him, venerates, and esteems him; and that she defers to him, praises him, and loves and admires him exceedingly" (AMP). In this verse we are called to respect our husbands, simply because they are in a position of authority over us.

It's easy to respect our husbands when they earn our respect by doing noble deeds. But many husbands fail at times to do things worthy of recognition—and some deliberately act and speak in ways that demean and dishonor their wives and families. How can you treat a disrespectful husband with honor?

I believe the battle for respect is won or lost in the mind. Do any of the following thoughts sound familiar?

- *My husband isn't living for the Lord. His life shows contempt for God. His words and actions are sometimes slanderous. God can't possibly expect me to respect this man.*
- *He appears to be such a saint at church, but I know what he's like at home. How can I honestly show respect outside our home,*

when he's disrespectful, rude, and ungodly to his family behind closed doors?

- *Sure, Jim is a great guy and treats me and the kids well, but he's out to lunch when it comes to the most important thing in life—a relationship with God. How can I respect him when he's not looking to God for direction and guidance about our marriage or our kids?*

If you've had thoughts like these, I can guarantee that you will struggle to show your husband respect.

Can you respect a man whose life is out of order spiritually? Yes, and you should! Even if the spiritual part of your husband is out of sync (which usually affects other areas), you likely can find earthly good in him. You may feel like you're mining for gold, but the result will be well worth the effort.

Keep in mind that there is more to your husband than the spiritual aspect of his being—remember, each of us has five aspects: spiritual, mental, emotional, social, and physical. Just because your husband's spiritual life is less than perfect, don't discount his strengths.

If you want your kids to grow up to become godly adults, you'll make certain they see you obeying God's commands, including this one. So if you, like many spiritually single moms, have struggled in this area, I encourage you to try the following exercises.

Examine your husband's negative qualities and commit them to God. Take a moment to study your husband's weaknesses, remembering you can't change him (you can't change anyone but yourself). Here is a short list of some of the things wives I've worked with have committed to God regarding their husbands: a fiery temper, laziness, grumpiness, unkind words, messiness, over-spending, lying ... and even "biggies" such as unfaithfulness, addiction, and verbal abuse. While there will be times when a wife must speak the truth in love to resolve a serious marital issue, God is the one to do the true convicting work in the husband's heart and to help him change from within.

Examine your husband's strengths, and focus on them. Because I regularly need to remind myself of Rich's strengths so that I focus on the good in him, I keep a paper taped in the back of my Bible on which I've written a list entitled "Things I Love About Rich." To give you an idea of what you can write, I've included part of that list here. Rich is: honest, assertive, attentive to details, intelligent, self-confident, responsible, decisive, loyal, generous, imaginative, creative, concise, clear-focused, self-motivated, objective ...

What are your husband's strengths? Write them down and review them regularly. When you think about your husband, intentionally fill your mind with the qualities on your list. Lest you think this is my bright idea, look at Philippians 4:8-9. "Finally, brothers, whatever is true, whatever is noble, whatever is right, whatever is pure, whatever is lovely, whatever is admirable—if anything is excellent or praiseworthy—think about such things ... and the God of peace will be with you."

Earlier, Paul wrote, "Rejoice in the Lord always. I will say it again: Rejoice!" (4:4). Why did he need to repeat himself? I suspect it's because this concept is difficult to retain. Notice that *rejoice* is a verb, an action word. We aren't supposed to think about rejoicing, we are to do it! Practice it. "No discipline seems pleasant at the time, but painful. Later on, however, it produces a harvest of righteousness and peace for those who have been trained by it" (Hebrews 12:11).

Remember:

> *Do not conform any longer to the pattern of this*
> *world, but be transformed by the renewing of your*
> *mind. Then you will be able to test and approve what*
> *God's will is — his good, pleasing and perfect will.*
> *For by the grace given me I say to every one of you:*
> *Do not think of yourself more highly than you ought,*
> *but rather think of yourself with sober judgment, in*
> *accordance with the measure of faith God has given you.*
>
> Romans 12:2-3

Guard your thoughts about your husband. When he exhibits one of his negative behaviors, deflect it to God. Remind yourself that God is working on your spouse, and turn your focus onto the things you love about him. This is mental warfare — God's way!

But with God's help we can win this battle. I remember a recent time when Rich snapped at me in front of Becky, then turned around and stormed out of the room. Because I'd practiced, my shield of faith was in place and I deflected the hurtful words to God. When I saw the fury in Becky's eyes, I asked her to sit down and process through the situation with me. I reminded her that Rich's battle isn't with me, but with God. We prayed for him and then took a few more minutes to thank God for the good things we love about Dad, which helped both of us put our minds back into a position of appreciation, love, and respect.

When we intentionally *practice* thinking about the good aspects of our husbands, we develop a habit of gratitude that can override our human reactions and emotions. The key is a day-by-day and moment-to-moment walk with God, as this helps us see life from His perspective. Jesus tells us how in John 15:5:

"I am the vine; you are the branches. If a man remains in me and I in him, he will bear much fruit; apart from me you can do nothing."

Can God build something beautiful from a couple if they are worlds apart spiritually? Yes! Hebrews 10:23-25 says,

> *Let us hold unswervingly to the hope we profess, for he who promised is faithful. And let us consider how we may spur one another on toward love and good deeds . . . let us encourage one another. (Emphasis added)*

Have you considered — with gratitude — your husband's strengths today? If you want to raise godly children, seek to build up their father in their eyes and in the eyes of others. When your mind and heart have the right attitude, your mouth will follow.

Building His Reputation

Ask yourself: What do others — including my kids — hear me saying about my husband? "The good [woman] brings good things out of the good stored up in [her] heart, and the evil [woman] brings evil things out of the evil stored up in [her] heart. For out of the overflow of [her] heart [her] mouth speaks" (Luke 6:45).

I'm not suggesting that you insincerely praise your husband. That won't build his reputation. Nor am I advocating that you go overboard with the compliments or ignore his sins and weaknesses. But you can speak honest words of gratitude about specific qualities and deeds.

When I first began complimenting Rich, my purpose was to edify him. But the good things I heard myself saying about him also encouraged me! I began to believe them and to feel better about him. In fact, that is one of the principles that brought the love and affection back to our marriage.

This principle works for others, too. Becky and I both need to hear people praising Rich—so that's what I do, for everyone's benefit. So, when the three of us are eating dinner, I might say something like, "Rich, the yard looks beautiful this year. Whatever you did with the fertilizing is working great. Thanks!"

Have you spoken positively about your husband to anyone today? Make the effort, for

> *Whoever would love life*
> *and see good days*
> *must keep his tongue from evil*
> *and his lips from deceitful speech.*
>
> 1 Peter 3:10

Maybe you could tell the women in your Bible study how much you appreciate your husband's thoughtfulness when he put the trash out that morning, or mention to your sister that your spouse put the kids to bed last night so you could do the grocery run alone. Hearing your own positive words will uplift your spirit!

All truth is God's truth. All good comes from God. The good in your husband is worth discovering and celebrating. If you base his worth on his spiritual condition, you are setting up yourself—and your marriage—for a fall. Unfortunately, many women don't understand that their husband's spirituality is not their responsibility. The wife often assumes the role of holding him accountable, which doesn't work and pushes the two of them further apart.

Let go and allow God to work on your husband's heart.

Someday, by God's grace, you may be one in the Spirit but, for now, do your best to meet your husband's earthly needs with excellence. Be his champion, his advocate, and advertise his worth to the world! Cheer him, comfort him, and radiate the love of Christ in your heart and your home. When a wife does such things, her actions can often influence her husband toward intimacy and understanding in their marriage.

Respectfully Submitting

But what do you do when you and your husband aren't seeing eye-to-eye on a specific topic—especially if his perception of the situation doesn't line up with Scripture? Perhaps one of the biggest challenges of the spiritually single mom is submission, particularly when her husband wants to go against God's principles. Unless your husband is asking you to do something that can hurt you or your children's physical or emotional well-being, I believe you need to creatively comply.

Not long ago a woman contacted me because her husband, a hurting and rebellious Christian, had decided they would no longer tithe to the Lord. He was also thinking about going into debt to begin a new project. She called me, wanting to know if she should submit to these ungodly mandates (see Malachi 3:10; Romans 13:8).

I told her "yes," she must creatively submit if, after reminding her husband about what God says about tithing in His Word, she is unable to dissuade him. I went on to tell her what I meant by this. Years ago when Rich told me that he didn't want me to continue tithing his income, I told him that I would respect his wishes. But I also told him I wanted the freedom to tithe out of my sporadic income, to which he agreed.

While God tells us to submit, this does not mean silently obeying our husband's every whim or ungodly desire. Quite the contrary, both husband and wife should freely and respectfully share their perspectives on a situation. It's important that our unbelieving husbands hear our appropriate words of truth, even if our words don't ultimately sway him to change his mind.

A friend in an unequally-yoked marriage recently told me about her husband's desire to take her to swing clubs. She asked me how to answer him biblically, and I showed her passages that speak of marriage partners protecting each other rather than sharing themselves with other couples. Instead of condemning, criticizing, or reproaching her husband, she went back to him with a firm, yet loving "no," *and* a promise to work on creative ways to make their intimate times very special—but private.

Remember that *how* you say something or *how* you do a thing often holds more impact than what you are saying or doing. With a genuinely respectful tone and attitude, you must speak truth to your husband when the Holy Spirit prompts you.

A lot of times we wives resist submission simply because we feel embarrassed or think, *How will it look if I . . . ? What will people think if I . . . ?* We cannot control how other people view us; we can control only our own actions. Since God has given our husbands the authority to make the final decisions in our marriages, He will hold our husbands—not us—responsible for the actions and reputation of our families.

In the Old Testament, Sarah's husband, Abraham, asked her to cooperate two different times in a lie to government leaders about being his sister—so that he would not be killed (see Genesis 12:10-20; 20). If even this man (whom God recognizes for his faith in Hebrews 11:17-19) could go astray and take his wife along, how much more might an unbeliever expect and demand from his wife?

When Peter instructed wives in the early church to submit to their husbands, he holds Sarah up as an example for us to follow:

> Be submissive to your husbands so that, if any of
> them do not believe the word, they may be won
> over without talk by the behavior of their wives,
> when they see the purity and reverence of your
> lives. . . . For this is the way the holy women of
> the past who put their hope in God used to make
> themselves beautiful. They were submissive to their
> own husbands, like Sarah, who obeyed Abraham and
> called him her master. You are her daughters if you do
> what is right and do not give way to fear.
>
> 1 Peter 3:1-2, 5-6

Clearly, God did not hold Sarah accountable for her husband's sin. This passage also implies that Sarah was *afraid* of what might happen if she submitted to Abraham. She had fears and anxiety just like we do, but her story and the following passages encourage us not to be afraid to submit to our husbands in obedience to God:

> For God did not give us a spirit of timidity, but a
> spirit of power, of love and of self-discipline.
>
> 2 Timothy 1:7

> There is no fear in love. But perfect love drives out
> fear, because fear has to do with punishment. The
> man who fears is not made perfect in love.
>
> 1 John 4:18

Even when the love a husband and wife share is imperfect, God's perfect love teaches us how to love without fear, and we can trust Him to love and protect us.

Here are some additional ways spiritually single moms I know are being creatively submissive:

- One mom takes her children to church every other week and the family spends the off-Sundays together doing positive, interactive things that draw them together—because Dad wanted to spend more time with the kids.
- Another mom arranged to attend Sunday evening services while Dad takes their daughter out to dinner or to enjoy an activity together. Then Wednesdays are the couple's "date night," while their daughter attends youth group.
- Instead of making mealtime prayers an elaborate event, one mom blesses the food with a quick sentence prayer and then spends more quality prayer time with the children at bedtime.
- A friend would dearly love to homeschool her children, but Dad wants them to attend their public school. This mom finds ways to be involved in the children's classrooms at school, and also teaches them about the Bible at home, at the end of the school day and before Dad gets home and wants to play with them.

You might be thinking: *Wow, Nancy, that seems like an awful lot of work. I don't know if I can be that creative. I'm already feeling like I'm on overload!*

That's why we spiritually single moms need a trusted, godly mentor to whom we can take specific situations, gray issues, and questions on how to respond as a godly, respectful wife. We can always ask our heavenly Father, but sometimes talking to a sister-in-the-Lord helps clarify our thinking and gives us a friend to share the burden.

Again, God doesn't ask you to submit to things that would be physically or emotionally harmful to you or your kids, such as asking you to watch a pornographic movie or the kids to join him for an inappropriate television program or movie. Even more important, if you think your husband's words or actions qualify as abuse, you need to protect your kids. *If your husband is sexually or physically abusive to your children, and you don't report him to the authorities, you may be held liable.* Go to your pastor or a trusted Christian friend and ask them to help you get help—immediately.

A Final Word

If you are reading this book, you most likely live with a man who refuses to deal with God on His terms. As a result, there are moments when your husband is selfish, mean, and perhaps obnoxious. Keep in mind that you too can behave in similar ways unless you follow Paul's directions in Galatians 5:25-26: "Since we live by the Spirit, let us keep in step with the Spirit. Let us not become conceited, provoking and envying each other."

If your husband does speak to you unkindly, remember:

> *A gentle answer turns away wrath,*
> *but a harsh word stirs up anger.*
>
> Proverbs 15:1

This verse encourages us to answer—not to put in our two cents, but to speak gently, lovingly, and for the good of our husband and the situation.

Most of all, never forget that God is wooing your husband to Himself. Whether or not your husband will respond to God is not yet known—but it is God's responsibility, not yours.

Strength

> *Wives, in the same way be submissive to your husbands so that, if any of them do not believe the word, they may be won over without talk by the behavior of their wives, when they see the purity and reverence of your lives.*

1 Peter 3:1-2

Strategies

- Our husbands deserve positional respect, whether or not they earn it by their actions and words.
- Commit your husband's weaknesses and sin to God to work on in His way and in His time.
- Try to avoid discounting the good in your husband simply because the two of you are worlds apart spiritually.
- Practice thinking about the good and rejoicing over your husband (see Philippians 4:8). This godly exercise truly helps override frustrations.
- When your mind and heart have the right attitude, your mouth will follow.
- *How* you say something or *how* you do a thing often holds more impact than what you are saying or doing.

Self-Assessment

1. How has your husband earned your respect?
2. What aspects of his personality do you not respect? How

have you responded in the past to these qualities?

3. What can you do to deepen your respect for your husband? If you haven't already made a list of his strengths, do so now.

4. How can you show your husband that you respect him?

5. How does your husband respond to praise, compliments, and words of affirmation from you?

6. In what areas would he like to experience more respect from you?

7. How is respect a deliberate choice and an act of obedience?

Speaking with God

Dear heavenly Father,
I praise you for the good in my husband that
you are showing to me.
I'm sorry for all the times I've focused on his weaknesses
and ignored his strengths.
Please open my eyes to additional things about him
that are reasons to respect him
and give me opportunities to praise and encourage him.
I give myself over to your protection and provision.

Chapter 4

Showing Jesus to Your Kids

When Rich first walked away from God, I was scared. I pleaded with God to bring my husband to his senses before Becky became aware of her father's lack of interest in going to church and in drawing closer to God.

As the years went by and Rich stayed away from church and all things spiritual, I became more anxious. Would I be enough to convince our inquisitive, growing daughter of the reality of God? Would her dad try to dissuade her? Would he attempt to stop us from going to church? Would she see Jesus? What would make her love Him?

If you ever experience angst like this, consider these two foundational truths:

1. You cannot believe for your children any more than you can make your husband realize his need for God. Each individual is ultimately responsible for his or her personal acceptance or rejection of Jesus.

2. As badly as you want your children to see God, He must

open their eyes, the eyes of their spiritual understanding. A child can grow up in a home with two committed Christian parents and still not "see" God. The Holy Spirit opens eyes, softens hearts, and convicts individuals of the need for God's grace. If you take every opportunity to show Jesus to your children, you must then trust God to work on the heart of each child.

These two principles release us from the debilitating responsibility we often unrealistically take on ourselves to win our kids' hearts for God. We won't—we can't. We need to relax. It is God's work in each individual life.

So what can we do to point our children in the right direction? Here are the top four ways I believe we can reveal God to our kids.

Have an Active Spiritual Life

The first several years of your child's life are the most formative, and you, the mommy, are the person with whom they connect on the most basic level. You can't show them Jesus if you don't know Him, can't see Him, or aren't drawing power from Him yourself.

Is your spiritual life active? Do you daily spend time praying, reading the Word, and meditating on the things of God?

I recently read the most marvelous description of meditation in Rick Warren's *The Purpose Driven Life*. He writes: "When you think about a problem over and over in your mind, that's called worry. When you think about God's Word over and over in your mind, that's meditation. If you know how to worry, you already know how to meditate!"[5] Warren goes on to say that we just need to switch our focus off of our problems and onto God and His Word.

I typically draw on God's power through key verses that I have memorized. As I pointed out in chapter 2, the Holy Spirit often brings pertinent passages to mind when I need them—that's one of His purposes for dwelling in our hearts. Jesus told the disciples, "the Counselor, the Holy Spirit, whom the Father will send in my name, will teach you all things and will remind you of everything I have said to you" (John 14:26).

When He brings a Scripture to my mind, I can consciously move my thinking from the troubling issue to the hope in God's Word. If I can't think of an appropriate Scripture verse, I focus on God and ask Him for help. I've followed this advice out loud so that Becky could understand the process and learn how to "renew the mind."

As Becky and I were driving home from church the other day, I caught myself in the middle of a worrisome thought. Just then, Becky confessed some anxiety, which mirrored mine. "Mom, I really hope Dad's over the ugly mood he was in this morning. It wasn't our fault he couldn't find the rake."

I admitted I had just been thinking about the same thing and suggested we pray together. I simply told God about our concerns and added, "I know you have not given us a spirit of fear, so Becky and I both claim your power, love, and sound mind (see 2 Timothy 1:7) and ask that you would give us a good afternoon together as a family." When I finished, Becky and I smiled at each other and agreed that we both felt better.

The more we know God and desire to become like Him, the more we have the potential to reflect His glory into the lives of our family and the people we significantly impact here on earth. It's not enough to fill our minds with Scripture, though. Our actions and reactions must reflect the God we want our children to see.

Mirror Jesus

A mirror reflects the image of the one looking into it. In His Word, God tells us He's given us His image. Imagine—we are God's image bearers! He has given us the potential to look, act, and speak like Him (see Genesis 1:26-27; Colossians 3:9-10). So, how well do you reflect Him?

Do you say and do things that reflect Him to the rest of the world? Do you care about the things God cares about? Do you help the poor and the widowed? Are you concerned with issues of peace and justice? When you compare yourself to what you know about God from the Bible, are you growing more like Him every day? That is His desire for you—to look more like Him every day in your attitudes, actions, and words, overflowing from a soft, pliable heart. Although we will be an imperfect reflection of God, our children should see aspects of God when they look at us.

Look For and Talk About God

I recently heard someone call creation the universal language we can use to tell people about God. The comment made me stop and think. *Is creation a language?* According to Psalm 19:1-4, it is:

> *The heavens declare the glory of God;*
> *the skies proclaim the work of his hands.*
> *Day after day they pour forth speech;*
> *night after night they display knowledge.*
> *There is no speech or language*
> *where their voice is not heard.*

Their voice goes out into all the earth,
their words to the ends of the world.

When your children are too young to converse about deep theological issues or too old to care what Mom thinks, point them to creation. The sunrise, the seasons, the mountains and rivers ... all of nature proclaims the great and awesome power and presence of the great Creator-Sustainer.

I've often used a profound spiritual activity called the God Hunt as a way to help Becky (and myself) become more aware of God's involvement in our lives and world throughout the day. Here's how it works. On a given morning Becky and I will challenge each other to a God Hunt. Then, throughout the day, we look for signs of God (something beautiful in nature, the smile and encouragement of a friend, extra courage when I have to do something difficult ...). That evening we compare notes and see who had the most God sightings. We both win at this game.

You may never have heard of God sightings, but I'm positive you've experienced many. What the world calls a coincidence, I call a God-instance—a point in time when parts of a situation come together in a positive way. God is the source of all that is good, and anything that is good comes from His loving hand. So a God-instance can be something simple, such as a parking space close to the entrance of the building becoming available during a torrential downpour. Or it can be as incredible as watching an out-of-control driver head straight for your car and miss you by an eighth-of-an-inch at the very last moment. Of course, God can also be sighted when you get hit by that car, land in the hospital, and witness to your hospital roommate, who then accepts the Lord as her Savior. Watch for the good that comes out of potentially bad circumstances.

God is working all around us and can be seen in the tiniest details—but we must open our eyes and look if we are to see and acknowledge Him. Did He make that gorgeous sunset just for you? Maybe not *just* for you, but He's glad you were paying attention, saw it, and gave Him praise.

An amazing God-instance occurred in our family about a year ago. Rich, Becky, and I stood in our driveway as a neighbor told us that the people moving in next door were an older couple, of which the husband is a retired, professional ice hockey player. This might not interest most people, but Becky adores ice hockey, both as a fan and a player. I rejoiced in this proof of God's love for my daughter. Then, when I took cookies over to the new neighbors when they moved in, I found God had also thought of me—our new neighbors are born-again believers.

Watch for God in all of the details of life, small and large—and not just in outward circumstances, but also internal evidence, such as peace in the midst of chaos, God's perspective in the midst of problems, courage in the face of danger, and more. *Expect* Him to be there. Look for Him. We make a huge mistake when we discount circumstances to chance. When your kids are with you, let them hear you praising the Lord for God sightings as naturally as if you were thanking someone for a gift they'd just given you. God is accessible to us.

We spiritually single moms need God sightings—gentle reminders that He is mindful of our situation—because we do not necessarily get encouragement at home. When I spot a God sighting—directed at me—I feel as if God has just hugged me.

These words from Deuteronomy 6:4-9 fit our situation:

> *Hear, O Israel: The* LORD *our God, the* LORD *is one. Love the* LORD *your God with all your heart*

and with all your soul and with all your strength.
These commandments that I give you today are to
be upon your hearts. Impress them on your children.
Talk about them when you sit at home and when
you walk along the road, when you lie down and
when you get up. Tie them as symbols on your hands
and bind them on your foreheads. Write them on the
doorframes of your houses and on your gates.

In this passage, God instructs the Israelites to teach their children to love and obey Him, and He gives them practical activities to do with their children. What might we do with our children today?

- Memorize Scripture verses and passages together (see the list from chapter 5).
- Attend church meetings and children's and youth activities.
- Develop family devotional times and family outreach projects to help children see God's love acted out in practical ways. Some examples: a friend of mine and her daughter pack boxes for underprivileged children every Christmas, another friend and her kids volunteer in the church nursery one Sunday night each month, and still another family visits homes for the elderly and presents musical programs several times a year. (We'll talk more about this in chapter 7, "Teaching Them to Serve Others.")
- Plan special lessons that can teach your child godly truths. Perhaps at bedtime every so often use an object lesson to teach a truth. For example: a caterpillar to butterfly is like a sinner to believer—a "new creation" (2 Corinthians 5:17).
- Make the most of teachable moments by reinforcing God's

truth as it pertains to the situation at hand. One idea is to point to a healthy weed you pull out of the garden and talk about how even things that look good in our lives sometimes choke out the best things God wants us to be doing.

Keep a Blessings Book

Another way to help children "see" God and His activity in our lives is a scrapbook or journal where we record God's blessings. Many people keep photo albums or computer folders filled with pictures of memorable family occasions. Why not keep a tangible record of momentous things God has done in your life and the lives of your family members?

Someone suggested this idea to my cousin Linda when her children were very small. She found a blank book and every night before she went to sleep she began writing down five positive things that had happened during the day. No matter how tired, she wrote five entries before turning out the light and going to sleep. She found that this simple exercise focused her thoughts on the good things that happened. An added benefit is the memory book she now treasures, filled with those blessings she faithfully recorded.

When Becky was seven, I encouraged her to do something similar. One day she came to me and confided that she wasn't sure God existed any more. She wanted to know if there was a way that she could be sure. So together we read Jeremiah 29:13, where God tells us that if we seek Him with all our hearts, we will find Him. He wants us to find Him, know Him, and love Him. In verse twelve, God also says He will answer our prayers.

I also suggested that she write her prayer requests on separate little flower-shaped pieces of construction paper. I told her that whenever God answered one of her prayer requests, we would "plant" the flower in her garden of faith. Every night before she went to bed, we prayed about each little flower's request.

By the end of the first week, five of Becky's prayers had been answered, and she wanted to begin her garden on the ceiling of her bedroom, where she could read the answered requests from her bed. The flowers we put up said things such as "help Miss K get well," "my friend to be nice to me again," and "no rain on my fieldtrip." Not every answer over the next several weeks was a "yes." Some were "no," and other requests were answered differently from the way we had prayed. One of her prayer requests was that her grandfather would be healed. When God took Papa home to heaven, with the faith of a child, Becky told me to stick that flower on the ceiling, "because he's just fine now—he's in heaven!"

We were both amazed when, by the end of one month, she had twenty flowers in her garden of faith—including one that read, "I want to know you more." As Becky's garden grew, so did her faith. She was "seeing" God work in her life and in the world around her by taking care of things she committed to Him each day.

Ever since Becky was twelve, she and I have met weekly for prayer. We write down the week's prayer requests on the left page of our individual notebooks and share them with each other. The following week, on the right-hand page, across from each request, we jot down what God did about each issue or situation. Over the weeks, months, and now years, our notebooks have become filled with tangible proof that God exists. After all, we can't see the wind, but we know it's there because of what it does.

Celebrate Spiritual Milestones

While looking for everyday proof of God is a great way to "see" Him, we can also create special occasions and make seasonal memories. When life is hard, celebrating becomes more necessary than ever, particularly if we are feeling weary, stressed, or lonely. As spiritually single moms we need to celebrate the positive aspects of life and emphasize this side of life to our children. Celebrations keep our focus upbeat.

On Mother's Day 1991, Rich (before he turned away from God) and I invited family and close friends home for dinner following Becky's baby dedication. After we ate, we gathered everyone next to our front walkway and "planted" a large, white rock in our flowerbed by the front lamppost. This *rock of remembrance* (see Joshua 24:27; 1 Samuel 7:12) still reminds family and friends to pray for Becky's salvation and devotion to God every time they see the white rock.

In Joshua 4:1-9, we read about God directing Joshua to build a memorial pile of stones that would be a reminder to future generations of Jews that God had miraculously brought His people across the Jordan River on dry ground. Verse nine says, "Joshua set up the twelve stones that had been in the middle of the Jordan at the spot where the priests who carried the ark of the covenant had stood. And they are there to this day." Wouldn't it have been fun to listen to a little grandchild years later ask his grandfather to tell him why that pile of rocks was there in that place!

What kinds of special *spiritual* occasions and victories can you celebrate in your children's lives, and how might you do so? Think of how you celebrate special occasions, such as birthdays (balloons, cake, presents), a lost tooth (the tooth fairy brings some money), or a good report card (maybe a treat, a gift, or a special activity). You can do these same things as a way of creating spiritual mile markers for your kids. In addition, always tell your child, "I'm thankful that God helped you do this great thing!"

Another way to celebrate these milestones is to buy or make a celebration plate that a child gets to use for dinner on a special occasion—such as his or her spiritual birthday, when he or she recites an assigned passage of the Bible by memory, when a family member makes a sighting of "spiritual fruit" in that child's life, when he or she leads a friend to the Lord, and so on.

Also include God and give Him thanks and praise when celebrating important occasions or events in your child's life, such as birthdays, graduations (elementary school, junior high, high school), the "keys ceremony" (when the teen passes his or her driver's test), or sports team championships. Sometime during the day of celebration, even if it is the last thing before we go to bed, Becky and I try to remember to stop and thank God for allowing and providing a way for her to reach this accomplishment. We don't want to make others think we make every occasion an outwardly "religious" time—this could annoy Dad—but we want to be sure to give God the credit He deserves.

But what if, despite your best efforts, your husband does act irritated or even makes hurtful comments to you or the children about the God-things in your life?

If Dad Resists Your Attempts to Show Them Jesus

Has your husband ever criticized your attempts to show Jesus to your children, accusing you of trying to indoctrinate the kids "with religion"? If so, gently remind him that each and every person—child or adult—is given a free will and ultimately chooses his or her own beliefs. Tell him it is not your intent to indoctrinate, but simply to teach the truth of what you believe.

If your husband gives you the freedom to worship (I hope he does!), be sure to thank him, and ask him to give the children an opportunity to know and understand what you believe, regardless of whether or not they ultimately accept it.

If he says "no" to the rest of the family attending church and other spiritual activities, your situation is similar to that of Christians who live in foreign countries where practicing Christianity is illegal. In those places, Christians meet secretly in small groups to read God's Word (or rehearse it from memory if they have no Bibles)—and of all the Christians on earth, they are probably the most zealous because of their persecution. Even though Rich is not hostile to the gospel, Becky and I will play praise music and talk about God more freely when he's not at home.

All of us need the encouragement of knowing others are praying for us. If your husband is openly resentful toward spiritual matters, keep a low profile but don't forsake meeting together with your kids to worship, pray, and read God's Word. Ask choice Christian family members and friends to pray for you and your family. *Keep praying and trusting!*

Stop, Look, Listen

Regardless of the creative activities you use to show God to your children, never forget that your life speaks most eloquently. You can participate in exciting God Hunts, make gorgeous memory books, and plan incredible celebrations, but if you aren't living a life consistent with the God you want your children to see—they won't.

When we get caught up in everyday frustrations, we take our eyes off God. Busyness, stress, or calamity overwhelm us, and our peace vanishes and we cease reflecting Him. Indeed, a few moments of anger can do great damage.

Think a moment about the difference between busyness and stillness. Busyness is about doing, while stillness is the absence of activity — it is a state of being. Are you doing all the right things *for* God, but not doing them out of a relationship with Him?

How can we live like Jesus without His help? We can't. Stop trying, be still, and allow Him to demonstrate His power to you and through you. If *you* haven't "seen" Jesus lately, be still — stop, look, and listen. He's there, waiting for you to find Him.

Strength

> *"You will seek me and find me when you seek me*
> *with all your heart."*
>
> Jeremiah 29:13

Strategies

- You can't point Jesus out to your children if you don't see Him first.
- Get in the habit of verbally praising the Lord for each God sighting in the presence of your kids; it should become as natural as thanking someone for a gift.
- Keep a tangible record of momentous things God has done for your family.
- Celebrate your children's spiritual triumphs.
- Apply your creativity to come up with spiritual mile markers and ways to tell your children you're thankful that God helped them do this great thing.

- Regardless of the creative activities you use to show God to your children, remember that *your life* speaks most eloquently.

Self-Assessment

1. What has God done in your life and the world around you in the past week?

2. What does God look like? How do you perceive Him?

3. What does God look like to your children? (Don't guess—ask them to describe Him to you.)

4. What can you do this week to help your children "see" God?

5. How can you tangibly record God's activity in your life so your kids can "see" Him at work?

6. What special spiritual events can you celebrate with your children?

7. How can you diffuse the stress in your life so you can reflect God's peace to your kids?

Speaking with God

Dear heavenly Father,
I praise you for revealing yourself to me and to my family.
Forgive me for my apathy,
for not always actively and gratefully looking for your provision
and blessing in the past and the present.
Please open my spiritual eyes so I can "see" you today
and show you to my children.
I give myself over to your way of doing things in my life today.

Chapter 5

Answering Your Child's Tough Questions

Has your child ever asked a question that seemed impossible to answer? For instance:

- "Why doesn't Dad go to church with us?"
- "Why can't I stay home today and watch cartoons with Dad?"
- "How come he can do that and I can't?"
- "Why did Daddy yell at that other driver?"
- "If the Bible tells us not to argue and complain, how come Dad does it?"
- "Will Daddy go to heaven when he dies?"

If your child hasn't started asking questions like these, it's only a matter of time. Do you know the answers? Do you know why your husband doesn't go to church or isn't interested in God?

Let's explore some possible answers to these questions, and then move on to how to talk with your child about them.

Why Doesn't Daddy Believe?

Your husband may be interested in God but dislike church. As was pointed out in chapter 3, many men find church boring. Others have been disillusioned when they discovered that those in church leadership can do awful things—and sometimes no one else seems to care or even notice. Some men become over-whelmed under a pile of responsibilities too great for one person to shoulder. If your husband ever went to church, he most likely did so hoping to find a place where people would speak and act with honesty and sincerity, and where he could make a difference and have a purpose.

Unfortunately, every church is filled with sinners—saved by grace—like you and me. I once heard that the size of a congregation on Sunday morning tells how popular the church is, that the number who participate on Sunday evening shows how popular the pastor is, and that the few and faithful on Wednesday evening demonstrate God's popularity. People go to church for many reasons, even some wrong ones. Your husband may be just plain tired of church.

Or, he may not be interested in God or spiritual things. Each person, individually, must at some point see God, recognize his or her sin and subsequent need for a Savior, and confess an honest belief in and acceptance of Jesus' substitutionary death. Without the Holy Spirit's revelation and conviction, a person just doesn't "get it."

In addition, some personality traits or tendencies can make it more difficult for people to see God. It's easier to accept those things about God with which we can identify. It's far more challenging to accept those qualities that we don't share. For instance:

- John, a Choleric (key word: *control*), understands the justice and grand accomplishments of God but resists yielding control of his life to a sovereign God who doesn't show him everything.
- Craig, a Sanguine (key word: *fun*), appreciates God's creativity and grace but feels that God's boundaries and discipline squeeze the fun out of Christianity.
- Henry, a Phelgmatic (key word: *peace*), identifies with God's love and peace but struggles with a God who would permit war and suffering.
- Josh, a Melancholy (key word: *perfection*), admires God's orderly, systematic universe but simply cannot understand grace. He asks, "If God is perfect, how can He tolerate mistakes? If I have the all-powerful God in me, why am I not more perfect?"

Neither you nor I can answer for our husbands the deep spiritual questions that they need to ask God. Each of us is solely responsible for our own spirituality. For now, we can only seek to understand where our husbands are coming from, and then pray wisely and without ceasing.

Just as you need to know that you not responsible for your husband's decision about God, so do your kids.

Not Knowing the Answer

No one knows what is in your husband's heart—except God, and He carefully shares only what you need to know. "The secret things belong to the LORD our God, but the things revealed belong to us and to our children forever, that we may follow all the words of this law" (Deuteronomy 29:29).

If your husband tries his best to be honest and straightforward with your children, then the best answer to their questions about his faith may be, "Why don't you ask Dad?" Why give a second-hand reply when they can ask the primary source? However, if you think your husband is not able to give priority to the kids' questions, encourage them to talk to him another day.

If this sounds intimidating or scary—after all, what if their dad tries to turn them away from the God you want them to love?—remember that trust is the key. Trust the Holy Spirit within you to give you prompts about what to say when your kids ask the hard questions. He'll give you the words you need or the peace to send your children to their dad with their questions, if and when He knows that's best.

Let me give you a couple of examples of what I have taken care of myself and what I've encouraged Becky to ask Rich. One day Becky came home from school, distraught because Rich keeps a few bottles of beer in our downstairs refrigerator most of the time. She asked, "How can Dad drink beer when it kills your liver *and* the Bible teaches against it?" (She was learning about the effects of alcohol on the body at school.) I chose to work this question through with her because I didn't want her to mistakenly condemn Rich, nor did I want him to think I was the one who put her up to such thoughts.

So before responding to her question, I made sure we had privacy and that I knew the Scriptures I wanted to use. Then I talked to her about what the Bible did and did not say about drinking—with the emphasis on getting drunk. I assured her that Dad is very control-oriented and would never give up control to anyone or anything, including a bottle of beer. I assured her that I have never seen or heard of him getting drunk. I also reminded her we can't see into the future, but we can trust God, who is the only one who knows what the future holds. We prayed for Rich, and we asked for greater understanding in knowing how and when to speak to him about things that concern us. Overall, this conversation was a scary but successful growing time for Becky (and me).

I also remember another time when Becky asked me why Rich would not go with us to the special Easter program our choir was presenting at church. I had casually asked him to go with us, and he'd declined. But I didn't think he would be "ticked off" if she invited him again, so I encouraged her to talk to him. He explained to her why he didn't want to go, she accepted his reasons, and we went without him. No happy ending. But Rich's explanation did spur on Becky to pray for him more diligently and more intelligently.

If the Holy Spirit prompts you not to send your children to their dad with their questions, you will need to do your best to answer them yourself. I recommend that you:

1. Pray, asking God for comfort, wisdom, and the right words.

2. Breathe deeply, relax, and trust.

3. Validate your child's question and express your sincere desire to address this concern.

4. Make sure you understand the question. Go ahead and ask the child to explain what he or she means. Try to determine exactly what the child wants or needs to know and proceed from there.

5. Answer the question with the words God gives you.

6. If no immediate answer comes to mind, ask: "Can I think about that for a little while and get back to you later?" This answer satisfies most children, most of the time — and it helps them realize it's okay not to know all of the answers. Make sure, however,

that you follow through by praying, searching the Scriptures, asking for counsel, and then getting back to the child with whatever God gives you to say.

Every so often, your child will ask an unanswerable question, such as: "Why can't Daddy see God like we can?" or "What does Daddy believe about God?" or "Why doesn't God help Daddy believe in Him?" It's okay to tell kids, "I don't know." Remind your child that all questions are valid, but that sometimes we need to wait on God for the answer, and that there is a Day coming when we will see God and know the answers to all of our questions.

Pointing Your Children to the Source of Truth

In school we teach children to use dictionaries, atlases, the Internet, and other tools to research possible answers to their questions about the world. But where do we send them to learn about spiritual matters, such as who God is and why do some people believe in Him and others don't?

We need to point our kids to God, who is the primary source of truth:

> "No eye has seen,
>   no ear has heard,
> no mind has conceived
>   what God has prepared for those who love him"—
> but God has revealed it to us by his Spirit.
>   The Spirit searches all things, even the deep
> things of God. For who among men knows the
> thoughts of a man except the man's spirit within
> him? In the same way no one knows the thoughts of
> God except the Spirit of God. We have not received

the spirit of the world but the Spirit who is from
God, that we may understand what God has freely
given us.

1 Corinthians 2:9-12

All of us need God's Spirit—also called the Spirit of truth—to teach us all truth (see John 14:17, 26; 15:26; 16:13-14). He helps us understand the truth that God has revealed in His Word.

Are you reading the Bible to your children, teaching them to read age-appropriate versions, and helping them memorize key passages? (See the sidebars on this page and the next.) Are you teaching them to go to God when they need guidance? Are you helping them understand how He can sometimes use circumstances or godly mentors to direct us?

Not long ago, Becky was struggling through the process of

Kid-Friendly Versions of the Bible

• For young children: My Very First Devotional Bible (Zonderkidz, 2000)

• For children: NIrV Kids' Study Bible, Revised (Zonderkidz, 2004)

• For older children: NIV Adventure Bible, Revised Edition (Zonderkidz, 2000)

• For girls (Becky used this for a few years): NIV Young Women of Faith Bible (Zonderkidz, 2001)

• For boys: NIV 2:52 Backpack Bible (Zonderkidz, 2005)

• For teens: NIV Teen Study Bible (Zondervan, 2006)

• For teens (Becky's current favorite): NIV Backpack Bible (Zonderkidz, 2004)

Don't miss the "Biblezines"—all or part of the Bible in magazine format—*Revolve* for teen girls, *Refuel* for teen guys, and *Magnify* for kids. (Nelson)

making a decision about summer plans. Her grandparents' input and her father's recommendation were polar opposites. I refrained from offering an opinion, but gave her points for both sides of the decision and told her I would be praying for her. She prayed and looked for a special word from God in her devotions each day. Although in

A Few Suggested Key Verses/Passages for Memorization

For young children:

Genesis 1:1
Psalm 23:1
Psalm 139:14
Proverbs 3:5-6
Isaiah 41:10
Matthew 6:33
John 3:16
John 14:1
Galatians 5:22-23
Ephesians 2:10
Philippians 4:13
2 Timothy 1:7
Hebrews 12:1
James 1:19
1 John 3:18

For older children:

Psalm 1
Psalm 23
Psalm 139:13-16
Isaiah 40:28-31
Jeremiah 29:11-13
John 14:1-6
Romans 12:2
Romans 12:21
Ephesians 2:8-9
Philippians 4:4-8
1 John 1:8-9
1 John 5:3-4

this particular case the answer wasn't visibly written anywhere or spoken in actual words, Becky came to a decision she felt very peaceful about—peace is one of the indications we're "on the same page" with God (see Philippians 4:6-7).

When your children ask about intangible topics, such as Dad's spiritual life, the same principles apply. Take them to passages of the Bible that explain spiritual issues. If you don't know your Bible well enough to find the truths you need, go to your pastor or an older, godly woman who can point you in the right direction.

For example, if your children want to know why Daddy acts so mean sometimes, you can take them to Galatians 5:22-23 and explain that because he is not a believer, he does not have the Holy Spirit, who helps believers grow the fruit of the Spirit when we ask Him to do so. Or you might at some point show your kids the condition of the person who refuses to believe in God as set forth in Romans 1:18–2:16. This graphic rendering might be too intense for a young child—make sure you read the passage beforehand and pray. Definitely also read this next paragraph of hope that comes from Romans 3:25-26:

*God sacrificed Jesus on the altar of the world to clear
that world of sin. Having faith in him sets us in
the clear. God decided on this course of action in full
view of the public—to set the world in the clear
with himself through the sacrifice of Jesus, finally
taking care of the sins he had so patiently endured.
This is not only clear, but it's now—this is current
history! God sets things right. He also makes it
possible for us to live in his rightness.*

MSG

It's important that we teach our children to run everything
they hear and see through the sieve of the Holy Spirit and God's
truth, as we're admonished to do in 1 Thessalonians 5:19-24:

*Don't suppress the Spirit, and don't stifle those who
have a word from the Master. On the other hand,
don't be gullible. Check out everything, and keep only
what's good. Throw out anything tainted with evil.
May God himself, the God who makes
everything holy and whole, make you holy and
whole, put you together—spirit, soul, and
body—and keep you fit for the coming of our Master,
Jesus Christ. The One who called you is completely
dependable. If he said it, he'll do it!*

MSG

God is absolute truth and His Word teaches absolute truth. We
can depend on Him to teach us right from wrong if we are
spending time with Him each day.

Telling Only As Much As They Ask and Need

In our zeal to teach our children truth and help them understand God and His Word, we can go overboard. I know I'm guilty of throwing too much information at Becky sometimes—more than she can grasp or needs to know right then and there.

When I was growing up, my father, a professional photographer, always gave me camera equipment technically beyond my skill and interest level. I don't think he ever realized the burden he placed on my young shoulders, which left me with feelings of guilt and embarrassment. Are you burdening your children with too much information? Do you talk with them about your husband's spiritual struggle, your challenges as a mom, or the differences between you and your husband in your marital relationship? While you certainly need to talk with someone about such things, do so with an adult, not your sensitive children. When you are talking with your children about your husband, ask yourself: Am I saying this for my benefit or my child's?

Guard your mouth lest you say something untrue or inappropriate about your husband to your children (or anyone). Adding conjecture—what you *think* but don't *know*—is dangerous. The Bible asks, "For who among men knows the thoughts of a man except the man's spirit within him?" (1 Corinthians 2:11).

About twice a year I visit with my church's pastor of counseling, just to assure myself I have an accurate perspective on myself, my relationships, and my home situation. We recently talked about how much I should tell Becky about my concerns relating to Rich, and he gave me an excellent principle. He suggested that I limit our discussion to the issues that she brings up or things I know she has seen or been a part of.

As our children grow older, they become more able to handle

complicated problems and understand deeper issues, and we can be tempted to use them as sounding boards when we need to think through a situation or when we feel the urge to vent our frustrations or grumble and complain. But God is clear on how we should talk about each other:

> *A perverse man stirs up dissension,*
> *and a gossip separates close friends.*
>
> Proverbs 16:28

> *Do everything without complaining or arguing.*
>
> Philippians 2:14

So be careful about what you say. Here's a good question to ask before you speak: What does *this* particular child need to know *now?* Think of each child separately, because every individual has a different maturity level and personality.

In addition to being careful about what we say to our children, we need to watch our words in other ways as well.

Avoiding Pitfalls

We spiritually single moms walk a tightrope as we try to be godly wives and mothers. We want to say and do things that will quietly exemplify God to our spouses. We hope our children see Jesus in us and grow up to love Him. Then, just when we think we're doing a good job, we slip up—lose our temper, throw a pity party, or reveal just how frustrated we are with Dad at the moment.

How you speak *about* your husband is just as important as how you speak *to* him! Remember, respect is crucial in marriage and in the family. You and your husband exist in a partnership—no matter how one-sided either of you feels from time to time. Partners protect each other. Protect your spouse's reputation with your children—be honest, but also careful and respectful when you speak with them about him. May your words always come from a compassionate, not bitter, heart, a heart that is saddened by his spiritual condition.

When people find out that Rich went from youth pastor to agnostic, they want to know, "How did it happen?" Over the past fifteen years, since the day he decided not to go to church anymore, I've come up with some theories. I've even talked over some of my ideas with Rich. But I am careful not to share anything with others that I have not talked about first with Rich. When I do talk about him with others, I guard my lips so that what I speak is never condemning or disrespectful.

All communication in your family and about your family must be grounded in respect and love stemming from an unselfish desire to encourage other family members. As you talk to your children about God, their dad, and other situations in your family, keep attuned to the Holy Spirit. Answer only as much as is asked and always, always do so with loving respect for everyone involved.

Lastly and most importantly, when you finish talking with your children about their dad, pray with them about his spiritual needs. Let me interject that this prayer time is *not* a time to beg God to "fix" Dad—it's a time to bring Dad's spiritual needs to God and to ask Him to help you demonstrate loving patience while God works on him. Pray with humility, realizing that you have problems, too, and others need to have patience with *you*. Then take the opportunity for each person to praise God for something positive about Dad. This keeps your children's hearts focused on the God who knows all the answers—and full of "thanks in all circumstances" (1 Thessalonians 5:18).

Strength

*The secret things belong to the LORD our God, but
the things revealed belong to us and to our children
forever, that we may follow all the words of this law.*

Deuteronomy 29:29

Strategies

- Both you and your children need to understand that you are not responsible for Daddy's mistakes, sin, problems—or ultimately whether or not he goes to heaven.
- No one knows all the answers, except God, and He carefully reveals only what we need to know. We need to learn to listen and follow the Holy Spirit's prompts.
- An acceptable answer to your children's question about Dad is sometimes, "Why don't you ask him?"
- If your children come to you regarding a specific problem in your family, talk with them about it. However, limit your comments to their immediate concerns so that you don't talk with them about something of which they are unaware.
- Before talking with your children about their dad, ask yourself: Am I sharing this information for my benefit or for my children's? What do my children need to know now?
- Protect your spouse's reputation with your children—be honest, but careful and respectful as you speak about him.
- Guard your mouth lest you say something untrue about your husband by adding conjecture—what you *think* but don't *know*.
- Pray with your kids about their dad. Prayer and praise keeps their hearts focused on the God who knows all the answers—and full of "thanks in all circumstances."

Self-Assessment

1. Why is your husband not interested in God? Have you ever asked him?

2. Examine your heart and then think about your responses to this question: Do you feel responsible for your husband's salvation or godliness? If you answer "yes," go back and reread this chapter to understand that your husband's relationship with God is his alone. You can pray and may influence him, but the responsibility is his.

3. What difficult questions have your children asked about their dad lately? How did you respond? Did you feel secure in God's prompting? How might you have answered more appropriately?

4. What things do you need to remember for future questions that seem impossible?

5. Do you ever send your children to ask their dad?

6. How are you teaching your children to find answers from God?

7. Which of the pitfalls mentioned in this chapter present the most danger in your life? How are you going to avoid them?

Speaking with God

Dear Omniscient One,
I praise you for perfectly parenting me.
Forgive me for the times I parent my children
unwisely and selfishly.
Teach me discernment and truth so I can answer
my children's questions
appropriately, lovingly, and with respect for their father.
I yield my heart, mind, and mouth to your perfect truth.

Chapter 6

Raising an A+ (Attitude: Positive!) Family

Rich wants a dog. In the worst way. After going around and around for months with me about the pros and cons, he declared one day, "I'm asserting headship of this house and declaring that we are getting a dog within the next year." Becky cheered. I cringed. From bad pet experiences in the past, along with the fact that we spend much time away from the house, I can't see the need for a dog. I know how much more work a puppy will add to *Mom's* schedule. But we are getting a dog.

I could be a wet blanket, sulk, and resent my family's decision and jubilation. Or I can get my heart in tune with God's commands to "rejoice . . . always" (Philippians 4:4) and "be joyful always" (1 Thessalonians 5:16). The issue here is not the dog—it's my attitude about what my husband has decreed. While this might sound like a trite example to a dog lover, it is a major issue for me. But I chose to give over my desires and opinions, and allow God to work out this situation to His glory. He is already supplying peace.

But what if a husband puts forth a family edict that the kids don't buy into either? For example, consider this scenario. Your husband says, "Let's go canoeing on the lake today. It's a gorgeous Saturday afternoon." You would rather read a book or take a nap, Amy wants to go to the mall, and Matt was going to get together with his neighbor buddies for some street hockey. Everyone looks at you. Isn't that the way it is? Mom will bail us out, she knows we don't want to do that! How are you going to respond when you know Dad's idea is a good family builder and makes sense—even if you really don't want to do it yourself? Oops. You waited too long to answer. "That's it—we're going," Dad announces. The kids moan and begin their excuses. What should you do?

When this happened to our family a few weeks ago, I prayed for grace, turned my mind to the things I like about going to the lake, and then began to give Becky reasons to enjoy this special family time. I gave her the promise of another shopping time and reminded her of the things she enjoys about canoeing and eating a picnic supper at the lake. Out of Becky's earshot, I also asked Rich if she could take a friend, and his "yes" finally won her over to the fun, family time.

Does being Mom take work? Yes! Though I don't know why God created the home to hinge on us mothers, I've experienced the phenomenon many times. As the saying goes, "if Mama ain't happy, ain't nobody happy." When I get grumpy, everyone else in our family is out of sorts. But if I refuse to get overwhelmed, frustrated, irritated, or anxious, it has a calming effect on Rich and Becky, and they seem to take on more pleasant and agreeable attitudes, even through stormy waters.

Our attitude is the "how" of our actions. You know the expression, "It's not what you say, it's *how* you say it." Likewise,

"It's not what you do, it's *how* you do it." Attitude takes into account the motive—what's in the heart.

What's Inside Your Heart?

One weekend I felt particularly taken advantage of by my family. Rich asked me to run several errands for him, Becky wanted my help with a major school project that she had put off till the last minute, and for some reason the laundry bucket was extra full from the previous few days. I kept thinking, *This is my weekend! I'm supposed to be able to kick back and relax. But everybody wants a piece of me. Agh!*

I had allowed Rich's and Becky's needs and demands to sap joy and relaxation out of *my weekend.* Isn't the weekend a time to relax? The Holy Spirit broke through my grumbling and complaining to give me a brand-new thought. *Perhaps the weekends are my "on-time" as a mom!* As the truth of this perspective resonated in my heart, my attitude changed and I began to consider my evenings and weekends "on-duty" time. I actually started giving myself permission to relax on Monday mornings, so I could recharge and be ready for the week.

When it comes to our attitudes about the interests and needs of family members, let's allow Philippians 2:3-4 to be our guide: "Do nothing out of selfish ambition or vain conceit, but in humility consider others better than yourselves. Each of you should look not only to your own interests, but also to the interests of others."

Here are a few more Scriptures that tell us how to live as moms:

> *For you were once darkness, but now you are light*
> *in the Lord. Live as children of light (for the fruit of*

the light consists in all goodness, righteousness and truth) and find out what pleases the Lord. Have nothing to do with the fruitless deeds of darkness, but rather expose them.

Ephesians 5:8-11

[Moms], do not exasperate your children; instead, bring them up in the training and instruction of the Lord.

Ephesians 6:4

Let us not love with words or tongue but with actions and in truth.

1 John 3:18

"Whatever you did for one of the least of these brothers of mine, you did for me."

Matthew 25:40

"The most important [commandment] . . . is this: . . . 'Love the Lord your God with all your heart and with all your soul and with all your mind and with all your strength.' The second is this: 'Love your neighbor as yourself.' There is no commandment greater than these."

Mark 12:29-31

Love is patient, love is kind . . . is not self-seeking. . . . It always protects, always trusts, always hopes, always perseveres.

1 Corinthians 13:4-7

But the fruit of the Spirit is love, joy, peace, patience,
kindness, goodness, faithfulness, gentleness and self-
control. . . . . Since we live by the Spirit, let us keep
in step with the Spirit. Let us not become conceited,
provoking and envying each other.

Galatians 5:22-23,25-26

Keep in mind that the *Holy Spirit produces* these godly qualities in the heart of a believer. Do not become discouraged because you feel it is impossible to bring about these traits in your life—God works these things in you. This is *His* job. You can trust Him to do it as you spend time with Him every day and walk with Him throughout the day.

As He fills our hearts with these qualities, they will spill over into our lives. It works like this. Let's say I'm holding a full glass of milk and I get bumped. What's going to come out of the glass? Milk, of course. Why milk and not something else? Because the glass was filled with milk, not water or soda or juice. Your life is going to get "bumped," no doubt about it. The question is: what's going to come out of you? Graciousness or irritation? Anger or compassion? Jealousy or contentment? Worry or peace? What's inside of you?

If you don't like what you see, get closer to the Light so that He can fill your heart with godly qualities and help you see your world as He sees it. Ephesians 5:14 says,

Wake up, O sleeper,
rise from the dead,
and Christ will shine on you.

A simple change in attitude often puts out the fire of dissatisfaction and gives us a new sense of joy and peace (the fruit of the Spirit), and soon we're making progress.

Please understand, I'm not encouraging you to adopt an optimistic viewpoint. I'm talking about a transformation of the heart, which comes from the Holy Spirit as we spend time with God and seek to be more like Him. When our hearts are filled with godly qualities, we will have joy, no matter our circumstances.

While it is God who changes our hearts, that doesn't mean we can do nothing to change our attitude. There are some strategies that can help us lift our spirits and improve our attitudes. In the next sections we will look at how you can guard your attitude, laugh yourself silly, praise your way out of The Pit, and count your blessings.

Be on Guard

We have to guard our attitude because we can be tempted to take our focus off of God, and when we do, our attitudes can turn negative and life-draining. That's why Peter tells us: "Be self-controlled and alert. Your enemy the devil prowls around like a roaring lion looking for someone to devour. Resist him, standing firm in the faith, because you know that your [sisters] throughout the world are undergoing the same kind of sufferings" (1 Peter 5:8-9).

The temptation to give into frustration and negativity comes from three different sources: 1) the Devil, as these verses point out, 2) our selfish nature, and 3) the lie from the world that says everything should work out for us because we somehow deserve it. What can you do to resist the temptation to give in to negativity?

First, reject Satan and flee from him, calling upon the name of Jesus to deliver you. *God, in Jesus' name, I ask you to chase Satan and the negative thoughts from my mind.*

Second, confess sin and selfishness to God and "fix [your] eyes on Jesus, the author and perfecter of our faith" (Hebrews 12:2). *Father, I have been disobedient in wanting my own way in this situation — thank you for your forgiveness. Help me to see Rich's and Becky's needs and meet them joyfully.*

Third, daily read and memorize God's Word, and in so doing, enable the Spirit to bring truth to mind so that you can recognize the world's lies. "I can do everything through him who gives me strength" (Philippians 4:13).

These are two verses I've committed to memory:

> *A happy heart makes the face cheerful.*
>
> Proverbs 15:13

> *A cheerful heart is good medicine,*
> *but a crushed spirit dries up the bones.*
>
> 17:22

They remind me that I need laughter in my life, particularly if I want to maintain a happy household.

Laugh Yourself Silly

A few years ago when my many responsibilities threatened to overwhelm me, I found a much needed treasure: *Milk and Cookies to Make You Smile: Stories to Keep You Young at Heart.* Author Becky Freeman made me laugh aloud — and often! I would read one chapter in just minutes and feel recharged and refreshed.

For a quick pick-me-up:

- Find a book of short, humorous stories about whatever

stage of mothering you are experiencing right now. Allow yourself to sit down and read a chapter when you need it.

- Stop what you are doing, take a deep breath, and find humor in the situations or people around you. When life at home threatens to get the best of me, I often lie down on the floor and call out, "Pig pile!" which invites Becky to pile on top of me and leads to tickling, laughing, and all sorts of silly fun (this is even more fun with multiple kids)!
- Call a girlfriend and giggle over anything—or nothing at all.

Solomon, the wisest man of all time, knew the value of laughter. He said there is

> *a time to weep and a time to laugh,*
> *a time to mourn and a time to dance.*
>
> Ecclesiastes 3:4

Laughing cuts your stress. Take advantage of it!

Praise Your Way Out of "The Pit"

You know what I'm talking about. You've been in The Pit (and could be there at this very minute). We fall into The Pit when we feel physically sick, emotionally discouraged, mentally run down, or when our husbands make a thoughtless comment or our children deliberately disobey us. So we throw ourselves a pity party, and Satan tells us to party on and invite all our friends and family. He whispers, "After all, don't you have just as much right to be there as anyone else suffering from what you're going through?"

Don't be fooled any longer. Even if you don't feel like you want to get out of The Pit, know that God doesn't want you to linger there. God calls us to a life of praise and positive thinking:

> *Rejoice in the Lord always. I will say it again: Rejoice! . . . Whatever is true, whatever is noble, whatever is right, whatever is pure, whatever is lovely, whatever is admirable—if anything is excellent or praiseworthy—think about such things.*
>
> Philippians 4:4,8

> *Encourage one another daily, as long as it is called Today, so that none of you may be hardened by sin's deceitfulness.*
>
> Hebrews 3:13

> *A cheerful heart is good medicine,*
> *but a crushed spirit dries up the bones.*
>
> Proverbs 17:22

How can you praise your way out of The Pit? The very things for which you offer praise and thanks can become the rungs of the ladder God provides to help you climb out of The Pit. When you choose to obediently *fix* your mind on the good things in your life, God will *fix* your feelings. Someone once said, "It's easier to act your way into a new way of feeling than feel your way into a new way of acting." The feelings will follow—feelings that shape an attitude of willingness and courage. So choose to use the ladder of praise.

Praise comes in different forms. It can be joyful thanksgiving. "Be joyful always; pray continually; give thanks in all circumstances, for this is God's will for you in Christ Jesus" (1 Thessalonians 5:16-18). It can be telling God how awesome He is, singing songs of worship, or reciting His blessings and majestic character traits. We can praise God with our own words of thanksgiving, and when we don't have words of our own, we can borrow from others: open a hymnbook and read the lyrics to God or open up your Bible and read a psalm of praise or listen to your favorite worship CD.

The concept of choosing praise fits right along with living in God's presence so that He can light our way. If you are walking in-step with God and living in His presence, then you *are* in a place of praise. God, by His very nature, deserves and demands praise—He is worthy. Philippians 4:4 says, "Rejoice in the Lord always. I will say it again: Rejoice!"

In The Pit? Choose praise. Hand over hand, climb out of The Pit by using the rungs of praise:

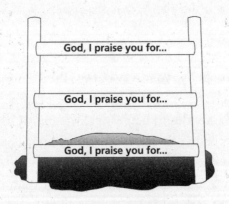

God, I praise you for...

God, I praise you for...

God, I praise you for...

Before you know it, you are out of The Pit, on solid ground.

God wants you "to be made new in the attitude of your minds; and to put on the new self, created to be like God in true righteousness and holiness" (Ephesians 4:23-24). If you habitually practice praise, you will become a woman of praise who lives above her circumstances. Your heart will be filled with "love, joy, peace, patience, kindness, goodness, faithfulness, gentleness and self-control" (Galatians 5:22-23), and your home will be a refuge of unconditional love—a safe haven of peace and acceptance.

Strength

> *Your attitude should be the same as that of Christ Jesus.*
>
> Philippians 2:5

Strategies

- "If Mama ain't happy, ain't nobody happy."
- Perhaps you need to consider weekends and evenings as "on-duty" times, and learn to find "down time" in other moments during the week.
- Your heart determines your attitude.
- The Holy Spirit produces godly qualities in our hearts as we spend time with God and desire to be more like Christ.
- Guard your attitude by rejecting Satan and fleeing from his temptations.
- Confess sin and selfishness so you can keep your mind fixed on God.
- Keep reading and memorizing God's Word, which is truth, so the Holy Spirit can bring verses to your mind when you need them to combat the world's lies.
- For a quick pick-me-up, find a devotional book of short, humorous stories about whatever stage of mothering you are experiencing.
- Praise your way out of The Pit.

How to Maintain Your Own A+ (Attitude: Positive!)

Here are some practical suggestions to help you maintain a positive attitude, even in a crisis:

- Practice God's presence and keep your life clean before Him.
- Take care of yourself—monitor the five elements of your person in order to keep yourself healthy.
- Limit earthly expectations and deliberately place your hope and trust in the God who is able to do far more than you can ask or imagine (see Ephesians 3:20).
- Make a concerted effort to keep ahead of your goals so you don't fall behind. Then, when a crisis arises, you are able to let go of the non-essentials in your day and focus on relaxing yourself and the people involved in the crisis.

Self-Assessment

1. How has your attitude affected your family in the past few days or weeks?
2. What is your normal reaction when things get tense at home?
3. What do you do to recharge yourself?
4. Do you make time daily to read and memorize God's Word? If not, why?
5. How can you begin using the ladder of praise? How can you have it ready for the next time you fall, trip, or get shoved into The Pit?
6. What are your biggest personal attitude busters? What can you do to proactively combat them?

Speaking with God

*Dear All-Powerful God,
thank you for giving me the power to think myself
into a better attitude.
I repent of my selfish attitude, exhibited so many
times in the past.
Help me learn to take better care of myself so I don't
live "on the edge" but instead can deal graciously with
everything and everyone in my life.
I delight in your encouraging presence in my life!*

Chapter 7
Teaching Them to Serve Others

Have you ever had any of the following thoughts when you heard a message on giving, going, or serving?

- *How can I reach out to help others when my own responsibilities overwhelm me?*
- *I can't do that! My husband would never stand for it!*
- *How can I give my time or money to the church when I don't have enough time or money for my family now?*
- *I've got my mission field right here in my home — why take on more?*
- *How can I serve the Lord without the other half of my team — my husband?*

If you answered "yes" to any of these, you have plenty of company.

Yet raising our children to be godly involves teaching them to "let your light shine before men, that they may see your good deeds and praise your Father in heaven" (Matthew 5:16). We need to show our kids that the Christian life is about serving the God we love — doing things for Him and in His name, to His glory!

Service is a natural outgrowth of our love for God. We do things for those we love. I enjoy making Rich's favorite cookies because I love him and want to please him. Although they may be tasty, the cookies are insignificant next to the enormity of my love for my husband. Somewhat similarly, anything I am able to do for God as His child is just a tiny, insignificant expression of my love for my Father. As we show Jesus to our kids and come to love Him more, we will want to serve Him.

In this chapter we are going to look at some of the reasons why spiritually single moms aren't involved in service, along with my response to those reasons. Then I want to introduce you to several spiritually single moms who have found a way to serve outside the home, with the help of their kids.

Why Some Moms Don't Serve

As a spiritually single mom, you may experience more stress than moms who have husbands who are their spiritual partners. You may think you are too tired to serve and that you have nothing left to offer others. If so, go back and reread chapter 1. It may be that your life is out of balance and you need to get it back in balance. Or you may need a change in perspective. I've found that when I help meet someone else's need, I get encouraged and strengthened. We get joy from doing the things that God has called us to do! I've also found that helping others helps me keep my own concerns in perspective — they are often not as overwhelming as I once thought.

Or perhaps you aren't involved in helping others because you think your kids are too young and inexperienced to do very much. If you think this, remember that God is probably not calling you to go back to the work you accomplished for Him before you had children. Something new awaits—some job that is as unique as the emerging skills and interests you and your children share. How exciting! God doesn't use all of our gifts and skills at the same time. Remember there are different seasons in our lives. Just as God gave exciting new endeavors in different seasons to the women described in Proverbs 31, He will do the same for you. Exult with Isaiah: "See, I am doing a new thing!" (43:19).

Maybe you possess great artistic skill, and, before having children, you helped your church and other Christian organizations with artwork, logos, and designs for printing. You think back to those fulfilling days and wonder how you can possibly fit even one tiny project into your current schedule. Instead of focusing on what you can't do, trust God to assign you something appropriate to do for the kingdom—something that will also include your children. For instance, perhaps you could use your artistic skills to be a part of the drama team at church. You could design the sets and your artistic daughter could help you paint them, while your outgoing son gets himself an acting role.

Or maybe you are hiding behind your husband, playing it safe. Maybe you think, *What happens if Dad doesn't go along with our plans? What if he doesn't like what we're doing or tells me we should be at home?*

If this is true of you, I want to ask you a question: Have you ever talked with your husband about any service ideas you feel God might be leading you to consider? If not, then you are assuming he is going to react negatively, and you need to talk it over with him. I've talked with Rich about everything of consequence that I consider doing. After all, if he allows me to do it,

I can be even more sure it's God's idea because God has worked on my husband's heart.

Or maybe you don't actively serve others because you worry, *What if I share my time and resources and find I don't have enough left over for my family?* However, the Bible clearly states that God's call is proof that He will supply the resources:

> *I thank Christ Jesus our Lord, who has given me strength, that he considered me faithful, appointing me to his service.*
>
> 1 Timothy 1:12

> *The one who calls you is faithful and he will do it.*
>
> 1 Thessalonians 5:24

It can be both exhilarating and frightening when we decide to take on some kind of ministry. We have to step out of our comfort zone and allow God to grow us as we depend on Him to show us how to do what He has called us to do.

How Some Moms — and Their Kids — Are Serving

That's certainly the case for these spiritually single moms who are creatively serving God, along with their kids.

Carol volunteers every other Thursday afternoon at the homeless shelter downtown. She picks up her first and third graders when school dismisses and drives to the center. She and the kids go up to the mother's floor and join the childcare staff member who watches the preschool-age children of the homeless moms while they attend a two-hour counseling session. Carol reads books to the little ones, while her children play with the other children. They get a pizza on the way home and tell Daddy all about their day of "helping" when everyone arrives home a little after five o'clock.

Janet wanted to do something to serve with her two pre-teen daughters in their church, but the girls weren't "into" helping out with babies or little kids. Then she stumbled upon a church bulletin announcement requesting help with a Sunday school newsletter. She remembered that the girls had seemed to enjoy helping her with office work when they were younger, and soon the whole family was involved in putting together a bi-monthly newsletter for one of the Sunday school departments. The girls even cajoled their artistic dad into drawing a cartoon strip for each edition. Everyone enjoyed the family activity, and the girls felt good about giving something back to the teachers and church leaders who were a part of their formative growing-up years.

Elise already felt overwhelmed when one of the youth leaders pulled her aside and told her he thought her son, Brad, was losing touch with the youth group and might be getting involved with the wrong crowd at school. When he suggested that she and her husband encourage Brad to go along on the summer outreach project in New York City, Elsie reminded him that her husband didn't want to have anything to do with church. He encouraged her to talk to her husband and promised to pray. To her amazement, Elise's husband not only listened intently and agreed there was a problem, but he decided they should go along as chaperones for Brad and the youth group on the missions trip.

Cheryl and her four kids volunteered at the National Day of Prayer rally in their town park. She asked her husband, Michael, if he minded that they would be busy for a few weeks before and then during the big event. With his agreement, she and the kids dug into the work of helping distribute posters to local stores, organizing the food booth, and setting up the morning of the event. Although Michael made a few comments about missing them, he was the one who cut out the newspaper article about the event, complete with his family's picture. The kids smile every time they pass the fridge and see where their dad stuck the clipping.

I have my own stories of how Becky and I have served God over the years. One of my favorite memories is a trip we took a few years ago to Ireland—with Rich's blessing. He wasn't as interested in the ministry value as the educational opportunity, but God did some amazing things on that trip, including validating Becky's "ministry."

On the second day of our trip I spoke to a group of women gathered in a missionary's dining room. When one woman questioned me about how Becky handles tough stuff that comes up between her and her unbelieving dad, I suggested she ask Becky directly. After about thirty minutes of talking with Becky, the woman came back to me in tears and said, "Can she come and talk to my daughter after school today? She helped me so much, and she could help Ashley, too!"

I hope these stories have inspired you to serve God in some way. If so, be sure that you want to serve for the right reasons—out of love for God and as an act of obedience to Him.

Determining How God Wants Your Family to Serve

Follow this entire process of deciding how, when, and where to serve God. Imitate Jesus, who was constantly connected to the Father, and always looked with compassion on the people around Him. Slow down and look at the people who are already a part of your life—what do your extended family, church family, and neighbors need? Do your resources fit any of those needs?

As a part of this process of deciding how God wants you to serve, take an inventory of the skills, abilities, and talents both you and your children possess. Also look at the time, money, and other resources at your disposal. Does this list of assets give you any ideas? Maybe you and your children can stuff envelopes for a mailing at your church. If that opportunity works well for you and your kids, you could ask to be put on a call list for other times they have similar mailings or needs. Call your church and other key individuals and organizations that might be able to give you a list of current needs you can compare against your list of resources.

Ask God to guide you through your lists of resources and opportunities—but don't be limited by them. Look at what He is doing in the world around you. Sometimes God invites us to join Him in something bigger than ourselves so that He can provide what is needed and receive the glory. In *Experiencing God*, Henry Blackaby says, "When I see the Father at work around me, that is my invitation to adjust my life to Him and join Him in that work."[6]

Be sure to involve your husband in appropriate aspects of the planning and decision-making process. When Becky or I wish to become involved in a ministry or outreach project, we usually talk to each other first and pray together about the opportunity or desire (especially now that she's a teen). If we sense God's leading (for example: all the pieces seem to fit or He's given us a particular verse that seems in agreement), then we pray for the right timing and words to talk with Dad. One or both of us will tell him about the situation, and elaborate if he seems open to listening. Then we ask him if he thinks it is a good idea. Even if he's not personally interested in serving God, Rich is good at helping us think through situations that involve the family. I've been amazed at the number of times he has given me excellent suggestions on how to make a ministry idea better. Involving him in the decision process promotes loving respect toward him and encourages him to join us in the venture, even if that just means "approving."

Back up for a moment. Be sure to present the idea to your husband on his terms (if he's like Rich, that means being concise), and with the best possible timing (on his way out the door to work is not a good time to address these types of issues). Also, be careful of your attitude—no manipulating! Present the non-spiritual reasons as well as the spiritual reasons why this is a great opportunity for everyone involved. For example, when I approached Rich with the idea of taking Becky with me to Ireland on a ministry trip, I stressed the benefits of the educational, cultural, and speaking experiences.

What if Dad doesn't agree? If he actually says "no," then discontinue your plans. However, this doesn't have to be the end of your vision for this project. Maybe the ministry opportunity is a short-term missions trip, and God's plan all along has been to involve you as prayer partners for the team. You don't need Dad's permission to pray. Be creative and stay tuned in to God's heart concerning your desire to serve and the opportunities *He* has prepared for you. Remember Ephesians 2:10: "For we are God's workmanship, created in Christ Jesus to do good works, which God prepared in advance for us to do."

Once God opens your eyes to the good works He's prepared for you, then He will be faithful to give you the strength and endurance you need to serve Him and teach your kids to do the same. I am confident that you can place your faith and hope in Him!

I know you can do this, because God "is able to do immeasurably more than all we ask or imagine, according to *his power that is at work within us*" (Ephesians 3:20, emphasis added) for His glory and praise.

Strength

> *We continually remember before our God and Father your work produced by faith, your labor prompted by love, and your endurance inspired by hope in our Lord Jesus Christ.*
>
> 1 Thessalonians 1:3

Strategies

- Service is the "doing" that results from "being" God's child.
- As you show Jesus to your kids and all of you come to love Him more, service will be a natural response.
- Helping others puts your own needs into perspective.
- Slow down and look at the people who are already a part of your life. What do your extended family, church family, and neighbors need?
- Don't forget to involve Dad in appropriate aspects of planning, deciding, and serving.
- Serve God with good works produced by faith and prompted by love.

Self-Assessment

1. Are you too tired, too worried, or too afraid to serve? Why?

2. How might your kids benefit if you begin to help meet the needs of others and involve them in your service?

3. How does your husband feel about you and the kids serving God? Have you asked him or dialogued about the issue or the possibilities?

4. Is it possible you are busy doing things for God that He didn't call you to do? If "yes," what should you do about the situation?

5. What talents and assets do you and your kids have? How might you use them to serve God in your church or community?

6. What is God doing in the world around you? How do your abilities and resources fit the needs where God is working? What are you going to do about it?

Speaking with God

Dear Sovereign God,
I praise you for creating in me a desire to serve you.
I repent of not serving you when I should and, often,
taking credit when the glory was yours or
serving with wrong motives.
Show me the good works you have prepared in advance
for me and my children to do with you for your glory.
I yield myself and my family to your direction and provision
for our lives.

Chapter 8

Helping Your Family Connect

While you might be tempted to gloss over this chapter as just another lesson on effective communication, this is the name of the game for spiritually single moms. We are humans. We communicate. We speak what is in our hearts and on our minds. Our communication defines us and has a major impact on those around us. These communication keys are enormously important for our effectiveness as God-fearing women who want to transfer our faith to our family.

So, how can we learn to communicate more wisely? How can we speak the truth in love, according to the needs of the listener? Let's break it down. We must *speak the truth* (be honest); *speak in love* (be compassionate); *speak according to the needs of the listener* (be "tuned in" to the other person). Good news: even if you're the only one working to communicate better, life will improve!

Be Honest

Honesty is the best policy. Honest people are trustworthy people—we can believe what they say, we can count on them to do what they say, and we can trust that they are not telling us one thing and saying something different to someone else.

But more than just part of a code of ethics, honesty is a command from God. We must not only model this quality, we must insist on it with our children. Godly kids need to be honest with their parents, honest toward one another, and honest with God and themselves.

Let me clarify what I mean by *honesty*. In a court of law, one must swear "to tell the truth, the whole truth, and nothing but the truth." Stop and consider these words. If we are to tell *the whole truth*, then we will not omit some of the details. We will leave nothing out. If we tell *nothing but the truth*, we won't exaggerate or embellish. We will stick to the facts.

Take a moment and reflect on how your words measure up to this definition.

Have you ever told your kids things like, "We'll go out for ice cream a little later," only to have something come up and it's bedtime before you even remember what you said? If so, you probably told yourself, *It's no big deal. After all, all parents say things like this, and besides, I truly mean to do what I say, so it's not like I'm lying or anything.* Sorry, but that doesn't cut it. We need to say what we'll do and do what we say, so limit what you promise to things you can and will fulfill.

Have you ever promised consequences for bad behavior but failed to carry out the punishment when the deed was committed? I cringe every time I hear a friend scold her children. She usually ends up saying something ridiculous like, "If you touch your sister again, I'll tie your fingers together." No, she doesn't carry out her threats. So, yes, the little boy continues to poke at his sister, who continues to whine. This mother is teaching her kids that Mom doesn't always mean what she says.

Do you let your kids know when you have been wrong about something? Everybody makes mistakes. It takes a secure person to admit failure and learn from it. Although it's preposterous, many of us act like we are right all of the time. But when we humble ourselves, admit our mistakes or sin, and apologize, we teach by example one of the greatest lessons anyone can learn: humility.

Exemplify humility to your kids, and perhaps they will exemplify it to others. I learned how satisfying this can be when Becky came home from school one day with a huge smile on her face. She told me she had apologized to one of the girls she sits with at lunch and asked for forgiveness for being rude the day before. She said the whole table of kids just stared at her, until someone said, "Wow, why would you say that?" She told them it's better to admit a mistake and get forgiveness than to have it eat you up inside.

Here's another question. If you were to ask your kids, would they say that you tend to embellish and exaggerate details, or would they say that you do your best to stick to the facts? Because so much of parenting is done by example, it's important that your kids observe you being honest with everyone—not just with them. Your kids need to observe you being honest with their dad, your friends, neighbors, and co-workers.

Spiritually single moms need to exhibit honesty, and we must require it of our kids. Rich and I both view honesty as a non-negotiable, and have made it a rule in our household: "Be honest." If Becky is dishonest, she gets a drop of hot sauce on her tongue (it brings tears, but a teaspoon of sugar quickly takes away the sting). The result: our daughter is honest, straightforward, and sincere.

Being honest is a top priority, but it is not enough. Blunt, to-the-point honesty can hurt. That's why Ephesians tells us to speak the truth *in love* (see 4:15).

Be Loving

How do you talk to family members? Whom do you love more—yourself or the person with whom you are trying to communicate?

First Corinthians 13, the love chapter, describes what it means to communicate love to our family. We should be patient and kind. We shouldn't envy a family member's skills and talents, nor should we feel superior because of our own abilities. We should never, ever say rude or crude things. We should stamp out our selfish tendencies, our anger and frustration, and the desire to keep score and advance *our* way over *theirs,* just to win. We should not say, "I told you so," while feeling smug. We should always celebrate the other person's victories and sing his or her praises, not feeling threatened by his or her successes. We must protect our loved ones, trust them, always hope and pray for God's best for them, and keep on complimenting and encouraging them in every possible way.

Remember Paul's words to the church at Ephesus:

> *Do not let any unwholesome talk come out of your mouths, but only what is helpful for building others up according to their needs, that it may benefit those who listen. . . . Get rid of all bitterness, rage and anger, brawling and slander, along with every form of malice. Be kind and compassionate to one another, forgiving each other, just as in Christ God forgave you.*
>
> Ephesians 4:29,31-32

Does this passage describe the way you speak to your husband and children?

In order to evaluate how well you do in this area, try this simple exercise with each person in your family, one at a time. I call this activity "Words I Say." Take a large piece of lined paper and put a name at the top of the page. Write down everything you say to that person until you have filled the page, then tuck the paper in a drawer for a day or two. Then get it out and read it—from the perspective of the person who was listening to you. What did he or she hear you say? What did you *really* communicate?

I did this assignment with Becky when was she about three years old. I remember being astounded by how many times I had told her to "hurry up." Was my child slow, or was I pushy? It took several weeks to alter my speech patterns, but I finally learned to encourage Becky with more positive word choices, such as, "Let's go, Sweetie" or "You have three minutes until we leave." Sometimes we lose touch with what we're saying and how it's coming across. We need to be aware and correct ourselves when we notice a problem.

In the midst of a conflict with a child, we parents often say things for our own benefit rather than for the child's. This is certainly true for me. Just yesterday, as I left Becky's room after helping her get started on a report she needed to write for school, I caught myself saying, "The mess in this room is driving me crazy!" I immediately realized what a foolish thing I'd done. Yes, maybe her self-discipline is lacking, but she was finally working on her homework, and I had just thrown on her the equivalent of a cup of cold water. In just a few simple, thoughtless words—with a negative, condemning tone—I had undone all the good I had done in motivating her to write her report. Yuck! I immediately apologized, but I could tell from my daughter's face that the damage was already done.

So I am learning to ask myself, "Why am I saying this?" If I'm talking simply to vent—I'm angry about the situation and I want it fixed for my own sake—then I am being selfish and my motives are wrong. James 3:2-10 speaks of the tiny tongue that wields mighty power. This is what the passage says to me:

> *My mouth seems like a rather insignificant part of my mothering "resources," but it can make or break my relationship with Becky. With very little effort—often just awareness—I can control my speech and use it to everyone's advantage. But I must remain vigilant and not relax my guard over this influential resource. Praise and encouragement is my goal.*

If you are beginning to realize you've got a problem speaking the truth *in love* to your kids—congratulations! Seeing a problem is half the battle. And fixing it can start with a simple confession to your child: "I'm sorry, Jeff, Mommy shouldn't have said that. Will you please forgive me? Let me try again." Then ask God for help to restructure your speech in a way that will edify and encourage your kids.

Another way that we can be effective in our communication with our kids is by taking the time to learn how to "speak their language."

Understand Your Child's Personality

Have you ever wondered how one set of parents can conceive so many absolutely different children? Fourteen-year-old Alice is quiet and thoughtful. Emily, ten, tends to talk before she thinks — actually, she talks all the time. Matthew, age eight, simply gets along with anybody. And preschooler Tara takes charge like she was born to be a general. Why the differences? It has to do with each individual's personality.

If you want to become a more effective communicator, I encourage you to learn all you can about the four personality types outlined by the ancient Greeks: Sanguine, Melancholy, Choleric, and Phlegmatic. Here's a brief summary of each of the four types. (If this information is new to you, I encourage you to read some of the books listed on pages 179–180.)

The Sanguine Talker. Sanguines talk *more* than the other personalities, but not necessarily more effectively. They "think out loud," meaning people around them know just about everything that's going on inside — a real plus for parents! But Sanguines also "tune out" easily because they get so tired of listening and because they are thinking of what they want to say next.

If one of your children is a Sanguine, love that child by understanding it's in a Sanguine's nature to talk a lot. Give him attention, acceptance, and approval whenever possible. Help him tone down the volume, listen to others, and stick to the vital details.

This child will naturally trust God and want to please Him. However, he might see God's Word as a book of rules that takes all the fun out of life. Help him realize that loving God is what makes us want to do what He asks. Help him experience God as being full of grace, mercy, and new beginnings by modeling God's grace toward others, particularly toward family members.

The Melancholy Thinker. Opposite of Sanguines, children with this personality type will not speak unless they are certain of having something worth saying, something that their listener will appreciate. When they are ready, they will share at great length with a myriad of details and support for their ideas, so accept their silence and don't pry. A Melancholy's comments can tend to be negative and critical, because this type is analytical. Melancholies are great "checks and balances" people. They communicate best when talking about factual, orderly details. They don't appreciate chitchat.

Laugh and cry with your Melancholy child; take her seriously. Sensitively encourage her to lighten up, relax, and have fun whenever possible. The Melancholy generally tries to be perfect about everything, and often can feel undeserving of a relationship with a holy God. Encourage your child to experience God's grace *and* give grace to others who don't seem to measure up. Help her realize that life is not all about *doing* for God, but most importantly about *being* God's friend.

The Choleric Doer. Like the Melancholies, Cholerics are task-oriented. But they tend to demand and order others to do the jobs at hand. Focused and intense, they are eager to get to the bottom line. If you have a Choleric child, be short and to the point in your communication with that child. Get to the meat of what you want to communicate and say it as concisely as possible. Then stop talking. Joyce Hulgus, a counseling professor who is a friend of mine, recommends a lean and brief approach instead of inundating the child with details.

Moms need to teach their Choleric children to be well-mannered (such as saying "please" and "thank you") and help them learn to focus on people (instead of the task at hand). Godly Cholerics have a godly compassion for people—and only God can do this in a heart. So pray *for* your child and *with* your child about other people. Prayer is a proven way to increase our compassion level!

The Phlegmatic Watcher. Phlegmatics speak only when they

have something of value to say, and they think and speak slowly and deliberately. They listen with interest and show enthusiasm with body language. Although hesitant to offer opinions, they often possess a quick, dry wit.

A Phlegmatic child needs your respect, encouragement, and praise. Give this child focused attention and wait to speak until he has completely finished a thought. Phlegmatics need a safe environment in which to express opinions and choices. Encourage your child to speak more quickly and loudly.

Help your Phlegmatic develop self-discipline and motivation that will keep him from procrastinating and spiraling downward in laziness, self-pity, or fear. And pray with your child for self-discipline, which is one of the fruits of the Spirit—something the Spirit Himself grows within us as we allow Him to do that work in us.

If you have difficulty identifying your child's primary and secondary personalities, try this test. Ask your child: If you were going to be in a play, would you want to be the actor/actress, backstage hand, director, or part of the audience?

- The actor/actress loves the limelight and has *fun* (Sanguine)
- The stage hand opens and closes the curtain at just the *right* time (Melancholy)
- The director *controls* the action by telling everyone where to stand and how to say their lines (Choleric)
- The audience member just comes and *enjoys* applauding for everyone (Phlegmatic)

Your children will not fit neatly into just one of the above categories, so watch for strengths, weaknesses, and tendencies that help you determine how much of which *two* personalities each child may possess. And *keep* watching and studying.

Be "Tuned In" to the Listener

Effective communication also requires that we be aware of the needs of the listener. When I need to discipline or correct Becky, I do my best to approach her in a *teachable moment*—when she is open to receive what I have to say. It's pointless to explain or correct children when they are not receiving our words. Notice, I didn't say listening, but *receiving*. These words mean different things. Anyone can listen to (hear) you, but a "receiver" internalizes what you say and processes the information, corrects his or her thinking and actions, and changes his or her conduct.

When Becky is teachable, her heart is like a freshly plowed field after a rainstorm. Seeds go in easily and take root quickly, as opposed to seeds in hard, dry, unprepared soil. A soft heart more readily accepts teaching so that it can take root.

One of the ways we can determine if our children's hearts will be receptive to our correction is by how they respond when caught in a wrongdoing. Are they mad, or are they sad? For instance:

> *MAD: Your son is angry that the person he knocked down went crying to the teacher about him.*
> *SAD: Your son is upset because something he did hurt someone else.*
> *MAD: Your daughter is angry at the person who broke her toy.*
> *SAD: Your daughter is sad because her toy is broken.*

*MAD: Your son is angry with someone who said
unkind things about him.*
*SAD: Your son is sad because someone is unhappy
with him.*
*MAD: Your daughter is angry with the tattletale
who turned her in.*
*SAD: Your daughter is truly repentant about her
actions and sorry she did wrong.*

A child who is angry is caught up in the heat of the moment, wrapped up in self. The child with a soft heart is sad because what he or she did wrong hurt someone else, disappointed someone, or caused a problem. This child is less self-centered, more others-centered. When a heart is open to realizing there is a problem with "me," then that person is ready to learn how to change.

It costs time and effort to know your child, read your child, and decide on the best words to communicate what that child needs. Praise God for His promised provision of wisdom: "If any of you lacks wisdom, he should ask God, who gives generously to all without finding fault, and it will be given to him" (James 1:5).

Are you a wise communicator? Pray with the psalmist,

*May the words of my mouth and the meditation of
my heart be pleasing in your sight,
      O LORD, my Rock and my Redeemer*

19:14

so that your aptly spoken words will be "like apples of gold in settings of silver" (Proverbs 25:11).

Responding to Your Husband

I want to close this chapter with one more aspect of communication that is vital in the spiritually single mom's home. How do you speak to your husband? What is the content of your communication?

The longer I live with Rich, the more I see the validity of 1 Peter 3:1-6, which says it is not a wife's responsibility to talk about spiritual things or instigate conversations with an unbelieving husband about issues pertaining to God. We are simply to practice our beliefs in our day-to-day lives and allow our actions to point to God rather than our words.

How can we know when to respond with the truth and when to refrain from saying something that might hurt, anger, or push our husbands farther from us and God? The answer is a thread that runs throughout the pages of this book: by relying on the Holy Spirit. Proverbs 19:11 says, "A [woman's] wisdom gives [her] patience," and 13:3 concludes, "[she] who speaks rashly will come to ruin." God's Spirit gives me wisdom to know when to be quiet and apply the principle "love covers over all wrongs" (10:12). So when I know Rich is angry or consumed with his own thoughts or perspective on a situation, I don't try to tell him anything because the ground of his heart and mind is not soft and prepared. Remember the section on children being "receptive"—it's the same with adults. Why speak if the words will fall on deaf ears? But don't use this as an excuse never to assert the truth!

The Holy Spirit also prompts me when I need to go to the wall over something and speak "the truth in love" (Ephesians 4:15). As a Sanguine, I naturally tend to speak more and listen less than most people, so as a general rule-of-thumb, I guard my tongue and refuse to confront Rich unless I know I need to say something. However, I know it's time to speak "the truth in love" when: (1) I feel a deep, personal peace, while at the same time hurting for the other person, realizing this is more his problem than mine, and (2) godly words of truth are in my mind, ready to be spoken.

In those times when the Holy Spirit gives you the green light to speak, be careful before you confront your husband. Never forget that the two of you are on the same team, and that you need to fight the problem together, not fight against each other! Listen carefully for the Spirit's still, small voice, read the Word, and seek counsel, for "in quietness and trust is your strength" (Isaiah 30:15).

We also need the Holy Spirit's guidance to know how to respond to our husbands. When Rich confronts or accuses me, I have to think fast in order to respond effectively. I try to call immediately on God for His perspective on the situation. I often run helpful truth statements through my mind, such as: *This is Rich's problem, not mine.* Or, *He is speaking out of his own hurt and I refuse to accept what he is saying.* Or, *He's right. I need to admit my sin, ask for his forgiveness, and work on this problem.*

A few months ago Rich took me to task for misplacing his hammer. "You were the last one to use it. You never return things you borrow," he said. I looked up from my work, pray-

Responding Under Attack

Does your husband ever say unkind things to you or the children? How can you respond in an effective, godly way? I often employ the following phrase, *with a tone of respect, not of censure:* "What part of that remark (or action) was supposed to be helpful?" This question, delivered with compassion, is designed to make the other person stop and think about what he said or did, and why. Another response could be, "What you just said makes me feel . . ." This personal comeback helps the other person become aware of how you are feeling or thinking.

ing earnestly that God would give me calm, sensible words and actions to diffuse the tension and be Rich's helpmate. I dismissed the later phrase because "never" made it untrue. But I acknowledged that sometimes I do forget to return something immediately. The bottom line was that Rich needed his hammer, so I got up to help him look, saying, "I think I returned it, but you're right that I sometimes forget to put everything away after a project. Let me help you look."

I had asked God to make plain to me what Rich said that was true and what was not. Then I rejected (put out of my mind, let go, refused to worry about) any untruth and set about dealing with what was left—finding the hammer.

The end of the story? Rich found his hammer with his secondary set of tools a few minutes after the accusation, just where he'd put it several days before. But lest I gloat, I admit there are just as many times I'm the culprit! All these situations give us opportunities to demonstrate grace.

To help you understand and communicate better with your spouse, let me recommend my book *Talk Easy, Listen Hard: Real Communication for Two Really Different People* designed for couples (but the book can encourage even one spouse who will read for understanding and practical tips).

The Bottom Line

God creates each person unique. So communication takes mutual understanding and work. But the effort is worth the sacrifice. Communication is a precious gift from God.

The first chapter of Genesis contains a list of what God created and on what day. At the end of each day, the Bible says that God pronounced His creation good. The only deviation is day six. Immediately after describing the creation of Adam and Eve, God *talks* to them. He talks to *us*.

Talking is paramount to a healthy relationship. In a spiritually divided home, relationships and communication are vitally important. How we communicate with our spouse and children connects us to them or disconnects us. Are you truly connecting with your family? Are you tuned in? Are you communicating honestly, compassionately, and wisely on their terms—for the sake of the kingdom? Make every word count!

Strength

> *A word aptly spoken*
> *is like apples of gold in settings of silver.*
>
> Proverbs 25:11

Strategies

- Speak the truth in love, according to the needs of the listener.
- Limit what you promise, and try to always follow through.
- Your tone of voice, choice of words, and even silences can be caught in the listener's radar—people often hear more than you realize.
- Enhance the communication process by understanding each child's personality and communicating in a manner that each child can receive.
- Look for teachable moments when your children are receptive and able to internalize and apply the concept to their lives.
- Expect to spend time and energy studying your husband and children in order to communicate on their terms—it's worth the investment.

- A wife's responsibility is most often to quietly practice her beliefs in day-to-day living, to allow her actions to speak *instead* of her words.

Self-Assessment

1. Are you honest? Do you tell the truth? Do you tell the whole truth? Do you tell only the truth? Did you try the "Words I Say" activity? What did you notice?

2. What are you doing to teach your children the importance of honesty?

3. What is your communication style? Are you a think-out-loud, gushing Sanguine? A quiet, thoughtful, analytical Melancholy? A blunt, to-the-point, concise Choleric? Or a relaxed, let-everyone-else-talk-while-you-listen Phlegmatic?

4. What are each of your family member's communication strengths and weaknesses?

5. Are you a wise communicator? If not, how can you improve?

Speaking with God

Dear God,
thank you for the gift of words and communication!
I confess that my words are often wrong, sinful, and selfish.
Please help me become a wise communicator,
listening to and thinking of the other person
above my own agenda.
As I look into your Word today, I praise you
for this precious gift
that gives me guidance, correction,
and encouragement.

Chapter 9

Setting Godly Boundaries

"Becky, it's Saturday. No school. Plenty of time to clean your room."

"Aw, Mom. It's not that bad. And I want to play outside. See, it's a beautiful day. Shouldn't I get some exercise?"

"Nice try, kiddo. But the room gets cleaned first. Now go. Do!" I gave my daughter a gentle push in the direction of her room and went back to unloading the dishwasher. Then I remembered I needed to change the laundry in the basement.

Back in the kitchen a few minutes later, I glanced out the back window to see Becky talking to our elderly neighbor. *She couldn't have cleaned up that room in such a short time. What is she doing out there?* I went to the back door and yelled, "Hello, Betty! Hey, Bec, is the room cleaned up?" She frowned just as the phone began to ring, so I hollered, "Get in here, young lady!"

Once the phone conversation ended, I went outside and explained to Betty that Becky had unfinished business, and then walked my daughter to her room. "I'm putting fifteen minutes on the kitchen timer. When the buzzer rings, I'll be back to check on your progress." I closed the door and went back to the kitchen, set the timer, and resumed emptying the dishwasher.

Buzzzz. I turned off the timer and walked to Becky's room. The door handle didn't budge. "Young lady, we don't lock doors in this house. Open up." Thud. Muffled stomps across the floor. Click. More stomps. Thud. As I opened the door, she lay on her bed glaring at me.

"I like my room this way."

"Right." I surveyed the clothing-littered floor, drawers sticking out at all angles, papers and books askew on the desk.... "Whether you like it or not is not the issue. I told you to clean up and you have disobeyed me."

"But, Mom, I'm more obedient than most of the kids at school."

She did have a point there. "But I'm not talking to the other kids. I'm talking to you. 'Fess up—you disobeyed me."

"But, Mom, I'm obedient about eighty percent of the time." She paused and then added, "That's pretty good!"

The truth in her statement hit me right between the eyes: *I am about eighty percent obedient with God, because I agree with Him most of the time. It's that twenty percent of the time I don't agree with Him that requires true obedience.* Wow. I stood dazed for a minute. Becky noticed, sat up, and said, "Mom, are you okay?"

I sat down on her bed with her and told her what I was thinking. We talked about 1 John 5:3, which says, "This is love for God: to obey His commands." I reminded her of the Israelites in the Old Testament who cycled through periods of disobedience when "everyone did as he saw fit" (Judges 21:25). And we discussed how hard it is to obey when the command or instructions don't make sense to you.

The most important thing we talked about was this: obedience isn't just for kids. We must obey God's commands for the rest of our lives. I pointed out to Becky that if she doesn't learn to walk obediently with me, she's going to have trouble submitting to God's authority, too. Then we both prayed, confessing our disobedience (mine to the Father and Becky's to God and me) and asking God to help us faithfully obey in every detail of life.

When I went back to the kitchen to finish unloading that dishwasher, my heart was lighter and my daughter was cheerfully cleaning up her room.

Obedience: A Spiritual Exercise

As parents we give our kids boundaries for two reasons: to protect them and to teach them how to discipline themselves in order to lead healthy, productive lives as adults. Our relationship with our children provides for them a model of how God, our heavenly Father, loves and disciplines us, His children (see Hebrews 12:7-11). Our rules and how we enforce them will impact how our children will view Him and how obedient they will be to His laws.

What can happen when kids grow up without appropriate discipline? When grown, they may rebel against God's loving discipline in their lives. But when we set appropriate boundaries and lovingly enforce them, we help our kids understand that God's commands "are not burdensome" (1 John 5:3). They are not meant to be hoops that we jump through like trained dogs. His commands, standards, and boundaries keep us safe, healthy, and free from the tyranny of self and sin.

However, we must examine our own lives before we apply principles to our children's lives. They need to see us obeying God so that we can effectively teach them to obey us—and Him.

Our Own Obedience

That said, how can we help our children understand the value of obedience when we disobey rules we don't like or don't agree with? We drive over the speed limit (government rule). We eat junk food (law of nature). We gossip and judge others harshly (God's law).

When I've disobeyed God, I sometimes let Becky see what's going on in my life—my struggle, my giving it to God, my confessing to God and to anyone else my sin affected—so that she has a tangible example of how we are to deal with sin and how to relate to the God who will forgive and restore us to a right relationship with Himself. I did this just recently.

For the past several months my hectic deadlines and special events have been keeping me from consistent alone time with God every morning. At least that's been my excuse. During our weekly prayer times, I've been asking Becky to pray that God will help me have consistent time with Him. Every week she has asked me how I'm doing, and every week I mumble something like, "Okay, but keep praying." Inside I'm thinking, *I have to get my act together so she doesn't think this kind of behavior is acceptable—I'm supposed to be her role model and she's having devotions more consistently than I am!*

A couple weeks ago, I came clean with Becky. I admitted that it's my fault I'm not getting up earlier and making time alone with God my top priority of every day. I told her I'd already talked to God and confessed my sin. Then I asked her forgiveness for trying to "look good" and not being honest with her. We prayed together and I made some changes in my life. Now it feels good to respond to Becky's accountability questions with, "God and I had an awesome time together this morning. I learned _____. What did you learn today?"

Your husband may not believe that we need to obey God, and he may be setting a poor example to your kids. He may not agree with some of the boundaries you want in place so that your children will grow up to become godly adults. Do not fear: God will enable you to handle the discipline in your home effectively, if you turn to Him for help. We have a God — hallelujah! — who helps us do what He requires of us. Not easy, but possible.

But our own obedience isn't the only thing we need to take into account if we want our kids to obey. As we consider how to enforce godly boundaries, we also need to remember who, ultimately, should be the enforcer.

The Best Enforcer

Some people would say the job of discipline should fall to the father as the head of the household. But in our society, a mom generally spends the most amount of time with the children, so she is the logical one to dole out punishment, especially when the punishment needs to fit the crime and must be enacted immediately to remain effective.

Whether the main enforcer in your family happens to be Mom or Dad, try on this idea for size:

> *Discipline should ultimately become the responsibility of the child.*

When I taught elementary school, at some point during the first day of a new school year, I would write three words on the chalkboard: *discipline, control,* and *punishment.* I would then ask for volunteers to explain how these words differ from each other, and I would guide the discussion until I had clarified the following:

1. *Discipline*—self-control—is what every child needs to establish in his or her own life.
2. *Control* is my job as the teacher, when my students are not disciplining themselves.
3. *Punishment* is one form of control, but many positive methods of control exist as well.

My goal as a teacher was to help my students learn to control their own actions. My goal as a mom is to help Becky learn self-control. Simply put, when our children are not able or refuse to control themselves appropriately, we must exercise control. If our children know this, much of the heat is off of us and onto them. If they choose not to control themselves appropriately, then they are forcing us to pick up the slack. If they don't want our control in their lives, they must provide it for themselves. (I started explaining this to Becky when she was four years old, which is the age when kids can begin to understand this concept.)

In *Discipline Them, Love Them*, author Betty N. Chase delineates the three stages of discipline that cover the child's development from preschool age to age eighteen.[7]

Stage 1—preschool to about age three or four. In this stage parents "stand against" the child. This means saying "no" firmly, lovingly, and consistently in order to establish boundaries and the concept of authority. For example, when my two-year-old ran ahead of me in the grocery aisle, I caught up with her and said, "No running ahead of Mommy." Then I enforced the rule by holding her hand or touching her shoulder when she looked like she might head off on her own again.

Stage 2—four- to thirteen-year-olds. Working with this age group means saying "no, because ..." and taking the opportunity to teach *why* they should obey. For example, "No, honey, you can't ask Jenny over today because we have a whole list of things Mommy already planned to do today. Let's find a time in next week's schedule when we can invite Jenny to come and visit." Sometimes "why" is simply "because I said so, and I know best right now."

Stage 3—thirteen- through eighteen-year-olds. In this stage, the parents "withdraw from" the teen. After working through the problem with a teen, the parent withdraws and allows the child to solve it on his or her own terms and to make his own decision. "Withdrawing from" is not cruel, but necessary. The teen needs to grow in his or her independence from you. For example, when Becky asks me to decide for her whether she should go to a school party, I encourage her to pray about the decision, come up with a list of pros and cons, and then come back and tell me what *she* thinks she should do. I make it clear that I'm more than willing to talk with her about her concerns, but she needs to start taking responsibility for her own decisions.

Remember, as children mature, they should become more self-disciplined and less in need of a parent's direct intervention. However, the development process is not a smooth, upward movement. Instead, one moment they act years older than their age, and the next you wonder how they could have regressed so drastically. That's one reason God put you in charge—to be your children's consistent guardian and encourager.

Children are not born with instruction manuals, but if they were, discipline would take up a large percentage of the book. Don't let anyone tell you otherwise! Helping your children become self-disciplined is one of your most difficult and time-consuming tasks, and a thankless one this side of heaven. Be prepared. Be armed with God's Word and His purposes for you and for your children. Then go forth in God's strength and wisdom. He can guide you as you seek to set rules for your children's behavior.

Setting Rules for Your Children

Here are some guidelines for how to effectively set appropriate boundaries or rules that can help your kids learn to control their own behavior.

Make a united front. Don't set a major boundary or rule without first talking it over with your husband. Even if you think he won't care, be prepared to explain, support, and clear your proposed rules with him. It's critical that your children know the disciplinary system comes from Mom *and Dad*.

K.I.S.S.—keep it short and simple! The fewer the rules, the less difficult it is to enforce them. Rich and I maintain just three household rules: be honest, be respectful, and be obedient. These cover almost every situation and they are simple for Becky to remember. Deliberate failure to keep any one of these three rules results in punishment. With honesty, we use hot sauce. With respect and obedience, we try to make the punishment fit the crime (for example: if she leaves her hockey equipment outside overnight, she puts it away properly the next day and doesn't get to play that day).

We are a bit different from a family with more than one child. With multiple kids, the house rules need to be set forth and enforced consistently to make life fair for everyone. For example, you may need to set up standard dating rules and curfew times, and so on. With Becky, we were able to help her develop her own set of personal "standards and convictions" (see Appendix) by which she would live her life. We help her stick to her standards, but she is personally committed to them because she's the one who developed them and prayerfully reasoned them out.

The other differentiation we could make is between rules and habits. Rules set the boundaries (be honest, be respectful, be obedient) and, when broken, deserve punishment. Habits are what we build. Habits are the good things we want to encourage in our children's daily lives (for example: being neat, being punctual, having good table manners, being polite).

Be sure to enforce your rules. Every family member needs to know the rules and be apprised of the expectations and consequences. You may be tempted, particularly when you are tired or stressed, to overlook an infraction of a household rule. This will sabotage your efforts to raise a child who respects God's laws and obeys them. Enforcing the rules is just as important as creating them. If you don't enforce the rules, you may as well not have them.

Adapt your interpretation of the rules and your expectations as your children grow and change over the years. When Becky was in elementary school she needed to have homework done and be in bed by nine o'clock. In ninth grade now, Becky sometimes procrastinates and doesn't start on her homework until later in the evening, and this moves her bedtime back significantly. I'm not as tough with her though, because she needs to learn to budget her time. It only takes a few late nights and a few days of falling asleep in classes for her to realize the need to prioritize her time more appropriately—*she* needs to reach this conclusion so she can own it.

The younger the child, the more firm, direct guidance is needed to help the child act appropriately. The older the child, the less direct intervention is necessary and the more the boundaries can be pushed out. Teen boundaries should be far less restrictive and rely on the responsibility of the teen rather than the parent. Teenagers must learn that as privileges increase, so do responsibilities, and failed responsibilities may mean a loss of privilege.

Lovingly correct them. Always love your children, even when you disagree with what they are doing. Above all, remain calm and consistent. Here are the three steps involved in correction:

1. State what is wrong and help your children confess it as sin to God and to whomever else needs an apology. Say, "Honey, what did you do wrong? Yes, kicking the dog is mean. You need to tell God about what you did."

2. Encourage them to tell you what should have happened. Say, "What should you have done—instead of kicking the dog—when you felt disappointed that your tower of blocks fell down?"

3. Love them through the consequences of their wrong actions. Say, "I think Buddy still loves you. Let's go over and pet him together."

If you feel insecure in the area of discipline, don't hesitate to ask for guidance from someone who's "been there, done that." Another resource for increasing your disciplinary skills is the nearby Christian bookstore. As you read, ask God to give you some nuggets of wisdom in the area of discipline that you can incorporate into your daily dealings with your children.

Going to Battle Vs. Showing Grace

As you likely know, the establishment of household rules can become a challenge in a spiritually divided home. While you base your ideas on Scripture, your husband may have very different ideas. Perhaps you want to limit the kids' television or Internet exposure, but he doesn't see the need for this restriction. Or maybe he just laughs when they occasionally use slang or sarcasm, which is something you'd like to forbid.

At some point you will meet resistance—from your kids and your husband. What can you do? When there is friction and disagreement, here is the key: learn to pick your battles.

For example, Rich is a stickler for punctuality—to him, punctual means ahead of schedule, not just "on time." This standard is part of his personal code of ethics, and he expects our family to follow this code. While I agree that it's important to be "on time," I disagree that being punctual means being early. However, it does Becky no harm to follow this rule, so this is not an issue that I have challenged Rich about. Instead, I've explained to Becky the differences between being late, being "on time," and being punctual-according-to-Dad. When we are doing something with Rich, we try to honor him by living according to his standard.

However, when Rich refuses to back me up in the discipline I feel is important for Becky's physical, emotional, or spiritual well-being, I pray and ask God if this is something to go to the wall over. At times God leads me to say nothing, as 1 Peter 4:8 says: "Above all, love each other deeply, because love covers over a multitude of sins." At other times He prompts me to go to the wall over an issue by "speaking the truth in love" (Ephesians 4:15).

For instance, a few weeks ago our family was watching television together and the programming changed to something I deemed inappropriate. I suggested that Becky and I go do something else. Rich didn't say anything, but he gave me "the look" that said plainly that he thought I was behaving like a prude. When I got up to leave the room, Becky remained on the couch. It was clear she had no intention of following me. Now that Becky is fifteen, she's at the place in her life where she needs to make calls like this based on her own principles, so I left the room by myself, simply to be a good role model. The next morning I talked with her about her decision, and how it squared with how she wanted to live her life. (There have been other times when I've told Becky I want her to come upstairs with me immediately, and I put on my "don't mess with Mom" face.)

Knowing when to choose your battles is not easy. This is something I struggle with daily. Do I bring up the truth, state it, and move on, allowing the truth to resonate and the heart to soften? Or do I camp on the issue and turn the situation into a learning experience for Becky? Or do I back off and give the issue to God and wait for a more appropriate time and place to say something?

Over the years, I've developed the following habits that I believe have helped me grow in my ability to make wise decisions about when to go to battle and when to show grace.

- I spend time every day in God's presence and consciously take Him with me throughout the day, because He alone can show me when and how to correctly facilitate a situation. I also keep short accounts with God (confess sin immediately) so that His power flows freely through my life at all times.
- I wait to say anything until I think the person is at least a little receptive.
- I try to remember to shut my mouth if my heart is angry. I know my words will come out poorly and disgrace God.
- I am willing to speak when I get that "spiritual kick" from the Holy Spirit—that sense of urgency that I must say something immediately.
- Sometimes I remind my child (or, in rare cases, my husband)

that I'm "on the same side." I'm *for* her (or him) but against whatever is wrong.

Remember, God has already won the war. So when major and minor battles still need to be fought on an individual basis, know that you are on the winning side. Wage war against the sin in your kids' lives with Jesus by your side. Through it all, love your children wholeheartedly as Jesus does. And walk with Him, as nothing speaks louder than your actions and attitudes.

Indeed, walking with Jesus is what you are teaching and modeling for your children. You want them, when they are grown and gone from your home, to discipline themselves to walk with God.

Helping Your Child Develop Godly Self-Control

As I've said, one of our primary tasks as parents is to help our kids develop self-discipline. One of the best ways I've found to do this with Becky is by teaching her key verses and passages from God's Word *in the context of her life* (so it makes sense and sticks in her mind and heart).

Several years ago, Rich agreed to accompany me to a parent meeting put on by our church's youth pastors. They encouraged us to parent proactively. Rich and I loved one particular suggestion. They said we should give our almost twelve-year-old challenges that would show visible accomplishment by the time she reached thirteen—challenges that would give her a sense of accomplishment by the time she reached her teen years.

So on Becky's twelfth birthday, we presented her with a list of twelve items in four categories—physical, spiritual, mental, and practical—that we challenged her to complete before her thirteenth birthday. Each of the items was an activity that Rich and I thought would help her make the transition from dependent child to semi-independent teenager.

One of her spiritual challenges was to come up with a list of "standards and convictions for her teen years." In this day and time, when the world substitutes "whatever feels good" for God's absolute truth, teens need to proactively identify and *own* God's truths *before* the world inserts its lies in their minds.

As she read books about what other Christians believe, I challenged her to find a Bible verse to back up each conviction she listed. Her final report represented convictions she's chosen for herself and proved against God's Word. Since that time she has begun living them out in her life—a solid foundation to help her swim against the flow of a restless, lukewarm society. (You can find a copy of Becky's standards and convictions in the Appendix.)

To celebrate Becky's thirteenth birthday and all her accomplishments, we invited over seventy of our family and friends to join us in our church fellowship hall for Becky's "Teen Triumph." We spent the afternoon giving thanks to God for her life so far and standing with her in asking God to continue blessing her life during these next *terrific* teen years.

How can you help your children grow up to be disciplined, have good manners, and act in accordance with the standards set forth in Scripture? It may sound simplistic, but your ability to succeed begins with *you*. You must walk in obedience with your heavenly Father first and foremost. Then, you and your husband (best case scenario) must come up with rules and standards that make good sense, enforce them with love, and trust the Lord for wisdom and courage. He will walk with you through the journey of teaching your children to obey.

Strength

> *No discipline seems pleasant at the time, but
> painful. Later on, however, it produces a harvest
> of righteousness and peace for those who have been
> trained by it.*
>
> Hebrews 12:11

Strategies

- Our heavenly Father's standards and rules for living protect us and give us a model for our own parenting.
- Without parental discipline, a child may grow up to rebel against God's loving discipline in his or her life.
- Obedience is most difficult when you do what God tells you to do even though you don't feel like doing it or it doesn't seem to make sense.
- When you are vulnerable and willing to expose weak areas or struggles in your own life to your children, you exemplify how to repent and relate to the heavenly Father who forgives and restores us to a right relationship with Himself.
- Whether the main enforcer in your family is Mom or Dad, discipline should ultimately become the responsibility of *the child* as he or she matures.
- Children need to know that your household disciplinary system comes from Mom *and Dad.*
- Keep rules simple and enforce them consistently. Suggested household rules: be honest, be respectful, and be obedient.
- Godly wisdom in our discipline comes directly from our close walk with the heavenly Father—wage war against the sin in your kids' lives with Him by your side.

Self-Assessment

1. Think of situations in your life that demonstrate your obedience to God and your acceptance of His discipline in your life.

2. Think about each of your children: how are they actively learning obedience? (Don't be fooled by the quiet, docile child who rarely puts up a fuss—look deeper into his or her soul.)

3. What are your household rules? Consequences?

4. Do you recall a recent time when you have shared with your children your own personal struggle to obey God?

5. Is your husband supportive, apathetic, or antagonistic toward the rules you maintain for your children? Do you talk about the subject together? How could you approach him and what would you say to partner more effectively together in disciplining the children?

6. How do you know what battles in your home are worth fighting and which ones should be ignored?

Speaking with God

Dear Father God,
thank you for being in control, while still allowing
me to make choices.
I'm so sorry for the times I have pushed the control
issue with my kids and
been dictatorial and accusatory.
Please teach me to set wise boundaries, effectively and
lovingly enforce them,
and respect my husband in the process.
I yield myself to your authority today.

Chapter 10

Enlisting Some Encouragers

I'm not the first to point out that life is imperfect. We all feel overwhelmed by obligations and emotions from time to time. However, we spiritually single moms often face additional challenges. Even if you have a terrific husband who adores you and your children, you can end up feeling like you've got more than your share of responsibility for the kids, at least when it comes to their spiritual lives.

Many moms try to be all, do all, and control all—to God's glory, of course. But even though it may seem as if everyone in the family depends on us to keep things running smoothly at home, we cannot do it by ourselves. We are not self-sufficient. God did not call us to be all things to all people. Instead, He created each of us as individual parts of the body of Christ. We each come uniquely packaged with specialized skills, abilities, and functions: "From him the whole body, joined and held together by every supporting ligament, grows and builds itself up in love, as each part does its work" (Ephesians 4:16). Each of us, with our strengths and weaknesses, depends on others in the body of Christ even as they depend on us. Together we do the work of the Lord.

Take note: Even if the all-powerful God lives within you, *you need help*. And help is available, and a part of God's plan. In fact, if you don't take advantage of the helpers God offers, you deprive others of the joy of serving and glorifying Him. Stop a moment and consider the resources God offers you.

Your Husband

We mothers tend to think that fathers don't understand our children quite like we do. Dads are often busy with work and other projects, and they have their own set of concerns. Maybe your husband wants to help out, but he already shoulders so much responsibility that you don't want to ask more from him. Or perhaps you shy away from requesting help because he's rejected your previous requests.

But if you don't regularly dialogue with your husband about the kids, you may be missing your best God-given resource. Don't overlook Dad's potential in one area, just because he doesn't measure up in another.

Case in point: As an agnostic Rich is out of the race for winning the "Spiritual Resource of the Year" award. However, his analytical, problem-solving skills never cease to amaze me, and I often go to him for help in thinking through a situation. But that's not all. Rich and I possess different personalities and perspectives. He often sees the details and the challenges while I see the big picture and can spin idea after idea off an initial thought. Most of the time when we work through a situation together, we get much farther than if only one of us tackled the problem. In areas where Rich and Becky share personality traits, he understands intuitively what she needs. The same is true in the areas of similarity that Becky shares with me, and here Rich often concedes to my suggestions or solutions.

Rich also knows me—my abilities and limitations—and what is going on in our home. From this perspective, he gives me wise advice about communicating with Becky and about whether to accept an outside-the-home opportunity or responsibility. I know Rich's talents and put them to use as I believe God intended them to strengthen our family. These situations provide me with favorable ways to appreciate and encourage my husband.

With God's help, consider how your husband's strengths fit the needs of your family. Do all you can to wisely and effectively incorporate him into the workings of the family. When he sees God using him in your life and the lives of your children, his heart may soften to the God who created the family to work so beautifully together.

God has also given you a resource in the body of Christ.

The Church Body

Who are your dearest friends? Are they believers? Do you have a network of like-minded people with whom you can share the entirety of your life, your deepest problems, and incredible joys? Do you have friends who will relate to you on the right plane because you are both looking at things from God's perspective?

Christians typically apply 2 Corinthians 6:14 to the relationship between boyfriend and girlfriend, husband and wife. However, I believe that our most intimate friendships should be with like-minded believers. We must keep the highest places of influence in our lives for believers who share our desire to live by the truth of God's Word and who encourage us toward God and living a godly life.

But it's not enough to surround ourselves with Christian friends. We also need to be part of a church body. I realize that spiritually single moms have many legitimate reasons for not going to church. I know firsthand that sitting in church alone sickens the heart with loneliness. It can seem next to impossible for one person to get the kids ready and out the door in time to get to the service, particularly if our kids are asking us why Daddy gets to stay home and sleep in. Help!

Exactly. You need help.

You *need* the encouragement, prayers, and help of the people in your congregation. Church gives you and your family opportunities to better understand God's Word, grow spiritually, be held accountable, and find spiritual encouragement, all of which refresh your spirit on a regular basis.

So make the choice to obey God and meet with believers as regularly as possible. As spiritually single moms, we may not be able to attend every Sunday. Borrow God's flexibility and creativity in the best interest of your family, but "let us not give up meeting together, as some are in the habit of doing" (Hebrews 10:25).

There are many Sundays that Rich would like to go Jeep trail riding with Becky and me or engage in some other fun, family activity. I've respectfully and clearly told him my conviction about going to church regularly (my goal is at least three Sundays out of each month). When I acquiesce to Rich's desire to do something once a month, my flexibility seems to soften his heart on the whole issue of church. On those Sundays when Becky and I miss church, we spend some time worshiping together. When Becky attends the Wednesday night youth meetings, Rich and I often squeeze in dinner out, often with some good communication.

If you don't have a spiritually strong partner, you can easily feel overwhelmed and lose focus on life and the tasks at hand. The right church body can come alongside your family with help and wise counsel. Organizations such as MOPS International, which stands for Mothers of Preschoolers, and Moms In Touch International (MITI) can provide additional support and encouragement. Don't go it alone!

While these organized groups offer support and encouragement, another form of support that perhaps ranks above them all is prayer.

Prayer Partners

Several years ago when I was considering a full-time ministry of speaking, singing, and writing, I sought the counsel of a godly woman. She told me she would be happy to get together and talk about how to get started—as soon as I had confirmed *at least five people who would daily pray for me and the ministry*. She said, "I've never seen ministry succeed without prayer, and I've never seen it fail with prayer."

As you and I seek to raise godly kids without the aid of our husbands, we most certainly need prayer. We need to pray daily for our husbands, children, and ourselves. We also need to enlist others to pray for us and our families (and we need to update our prayer partners regularly with specific requests and answered prayers).

I also believe that every mother—every person—needs a regular prayer partner (or small accountability group). Pray that God will show you the person of His choosing. (Note: sometimes the best prayer partners are not a close loved one or friend; they are often tempted to pray for your best instead of God's best. A prayer partner must be objective.)

Here's how it can work: Regularly share prayer requests and answers with each other. Commit to pray daily for each other and agree to hold one another accountable to do what you say you will do, whether it be to pray daily, exercise three times a week, or stop pleading with your husband to come with you to church.

Not every mother needs, wants, or is able to leave her home to pray with a friend at some other location. If you can't get out of your home, you can always pray together over the phone or via e-mail. Phone prayer is self-explanatory. If you are partnering in prayer over the Internet, you can simply e-mail your list of praises and requests to each other. When you receive each other's requests, hit "reply" and write out your prayer for the other person as you bring their praises and requests to the Lord. Then add your praises and requests for the next week and hit "send."

Some women—especially moms of preschoolers who feel like they are always "on duty"—need an opportunity to get away to pray at someone else's home, or at a coffee shop or library. The change of environment, absence of responsibility, and adult companionship breathe fresh strength into these moms.

If you need to get away, but your children are too young to stay alone, pray about talking to your husband about watching the children for a couple of hours once a week while you meet with a prayer partner. Many husbands agree to this because they can see that the time away makes a noticeable, positive difference in their wives. Others are more open to this request if Mom leaves after the children are in bed for the night or before they get up in the morning.

I deeply desire to partner in prayer with my husband. But for now, this isn't an option, and pining for something I can't have is unfruitful and further distresses my heart. So I recommit the issue to God and tuck it into the recesses of my mind.

I've been praying with my current prayer partner for over six years now, and we each keep a journal which lists our requests, answers, and praises. These journals (and the ones I keep for my time with Becky) give me encouragement and hope as I remember all that God has done in our lives.

One of the most necessary tactics in the battle to win our children's hearts for the Lord is prayer. As a spiritually single mom, you need to assemble the troops, and your front line warriors are your prayer partners. Don't walk alone when support and encouragement are so needed and available.

You might also consider the role that family members can play when it comes to nurturing your children spiritually.

Family Members

If you have Christian family members close by, consider asking for their help in showing what a godly home looks like or in nurturing godly values in your kids. Christian grandparents might invite your kids over for the weekend and take them to church, pray before meals, and share devotional times together. Aunts and uncles can take each of your kids out for ice cream and encourage them to talk about some of the struggles they are facing and how to solve them according to biblical truth.

If you have no Christian relatives nearby, I encourage you to find some local believers who would be willing to fill the role of surrogate aunts, uncles, or grandparents in order to help you meet the spiritual needs of your children. For instance, let's say your son's Sunday school teacher invites him to come over to his house on a Saturday when your husband is away on a business trip. Your son spends the morning fishing with Mr. Philips, and then they go back to the Philips' home where they collaborate on a small woodworking project. All day long they talk about stuff that concerns your son, and Mr. Philips listens, gives godly advice, and basically affirms what you are teaching your son at home.

A spiritually divided household needs these surrogate family members, so look within your local circle of believers for someone who is able and willing to step in and fill a spiritual or practical void. Consider asking a youth leader or an older couple in your church to spend time once a month or so with a child, come to special events and programs in which that child is participating in at church, and pray daily for that child's spiritual welfare. Help your kids get to know other "cool" Christians, which can enable them to see that Christianity is more than "just Mom's religion."

Caution! *Don't look for a surrogate dad.* Be careful to honor your husband's authority and his role in your children's lives wherever and whenever possible. Your children already have a heavenly Father and an earthly father. Look for surrogate aunts and uncles, big sisters and brothers, and grandparents. If you pursue this idea, monitor your husband's reaction. Do everything in your power to help him feel a part of every other aspect of the children's lives.

At Just the Right Time

In the fight for our children's hearts, we can't let down our guard, even when we feel exhausted. Our surrogate family members, prayer partners, and other encouragers can support us. They can help us hold on while God works in the hearts of our husbands.

Do you remember the story of Moses when God called him to preside over the battle with the Amalekites?

As long as Moses held up his hands, the Israelites were winning, but whenever he lowered his hands,

*the Amalekites were winning. When Moses' hands
grew tired, they took a stone and put it under him
and he sat on it. Aaron and Hur held his hands
up — one on one side, one on the other — so that
his hands remained steady till sunset. So Joshua
overcame the Amalekite army with the sword.*

Exodus 17:11-13

Aaron and Hur didn't replace Moses; they came alongside him and propped him up, at just the right time.

Your husband, the body of Christ, prayer partners, family members, and surrogate family members all play roles in supporting you and your children. But it can be difficult to ask for help. Most of us find it easier to lend a hand and help someone else in need. But remember that God created us to be relational, dependent, and encouraging to one another. God's family works together to give Him the glory, and has been doing so for a long time.

As I write this I am praying for you, praying that God will provide Christians to come alongside you and partner with you in raising well-rounded and godly kids. Please, don't try to go it alone. Seek God and His way for you. He can provide many additional helpers who can come along your path at just the perfect time, in just the right place, and with the special touch you and your family need for the moment.

Strength

*From him the whole body, joined and held together
by every supporting ligament, grows and builds itself
up in love, as each part does its work.*

Ephesians 4:16

Strategies

- Even if the all-powerful God lives within you, as a spiritually single mom *you need help*.
- Consider how your husband's strengths fit the needs of your children, and incorporate him into the workings of the family.
- Keep the highest places of influence in your life for believers who share your desire to live by the truth of God's Word and encourage you toward godly living.
- Be involved in your local church. Church gives you and your family opportunities for learning, spiritual growth, accountability, worship, fellowship, and encouragement on a regular basis.
- Enlist some prayer partners. One of the most necessary tactics in the battle to win your children's hearts for the Lord is prayer—and your front line warriors are your prayer partners.
- Aunts, uncles, and grandparents—or surrogate family members—can help you meet the spiritual needs of your children and help them see Christianity as more than "just Mom's religion."
- Honor your husband's authority and role in your children's lives wherever and whenever possible—don't try to replace him.
- Seek God's face and His way for you, even as you walk the path with others who faithfully encourage you.

Self-Assessment

1. What is the value of sharing with others in the body of Christ the responsibility of raising your kids to love God? Why is asking for help so difficult?

2. Think back over your life and identify the spiritual encouragers with whom God has blessed you.

3. How is your husband partnering with you? In what ways can you encourage him?

4. Do your children need the godly influence of family or spiritual family members? Who is God bringing to your mind to help them?

5. Are you going to church regularly? If not, why not and what problems must you overcome?

6. Do you have a prayer partner with whom you regularly pray? If you don't, who is God laying on your heart right now? Call them and start the ball rolling!

7. Different people need different types of encouragement. What or who do you and your children need right now?

Speaking with God

Dear Provider of my needs,
thank you for the encouragers you have placed in my
life throughout the years.
I confess I am needy, weak, and frail.
Show me where I need help today, who can help me,
and how to ask.
I yield myself today to your Spirit,
the One who provides help and hope when I need it.

Chapter 11

Letting Go and Trusting God

We moms often try to keep our world running smoothly by implementing house rules, creating chore charts, and establishing routines. Unfortunately our peace of mind gets interrupted on a regular basis by things such as an appliance breakdown, a call from the school nurse, a fender bender on the way to piano lessons, or a report card with an unexpected bad grade. In our attempt to stabilize our lives and environment, we sometimes grasp for control.

That's certainly been true for me. When I'm already feeling overwhelmed and my daughter challenges my authority or suggests an idea I feel is outrageous, I find myself shutting her down and insisting we do things "the way we've always done it." Instead of calmly listening to her, I react and lose the opportunity to connect with my daughter and to help her think through the situation and come to an objective decision. When our children's newfangled ideas make us nervous, it's easier to discount their thinking rather than to encourage them to think independently.

That's why it's important for us to learn what it means to let go and to trust God with our kids.

Letting Go

May I ask you a question? Are you allowing your children to grow up?

As spiritually single moms, we are particularly susceptible to becoming over-protective in our desire to guard our children's hearts, lives, and decisions. After all, so much is at stake. But we can so desire that they love God that we push Him right down their throats. We may try to protect them from their father's beliefs or lack thereof. Sure we may ask others in the church to help our kids learn about God, but the bottom line responsibility is ours, right? So we pray, we push, and we stress over our kids until they stress out about us *and God*! When they eventually get out on their own in the world, will they choose God or walk away?

In addition, our desire to protect our kids can cause us wrongly to enable them to walk through childhood without making any mistakes. Our child may look good, and we may look good and feel justified in saving our child from the painful consequences of making poor choices. But does this approach to parenting help prepare a child for the realities of adulthood?

I'm sure you've noticed that many adults are still not "grown up." I suspect that this immaturity often stems from poor parenting. When parents make all the decisions and keep cramped boundaries on the family, their kids enter adulthood suddenly, eager yet ill-equipped to make right choices. Parents need to give kids opportunities to learn how to reason and to make wise choices so that they learn these skills before the choices come with big price tags. If children don't receive these opportunities, they enter adulthood unprepared.

Life skills are learned through practice; they are not natural abilities. Practice means doing, doing, doing. Learning to do something well may mean doing it incorrectly, being corrected, learning from experience, and adjusting our thinking and behavior accordingly. Unless we give our children freedom to make choices—and mistakes—they won't develop the necessary skills to make wise decisions in the future.

So if you want to help your kids mature into independent and healthy adults who love and serve God, you might need to let go, little by little. After all, isn't that the goal of parenting? Our children are born to us as totally dependent beings, then eighteen or so years later they leave the nest as independent young adults. They don't suddenly and completely mature at the age of eighteen, but over time, little by little, step by step. Ultimately, our goal is not to control our kids' minds or to keep them from making mistakes, it's to help them become self-reliant.

Here are some guidelines to help you do just that:

Give young children opportunities to make small decisions and then give them opportunities for more complex decisions and increased independence as they prove trustworthy. God gave your children rational minds, decision-making abilities, and a desire to be independent. This desire grows stronger and stronger as they mature into their teen years. This, too, God intended in order to help encourage them to be self-reliant adults.

Parents can begin helping their children develop their decision-making skills when their kids are still very young. Rich and I began encouraging Becky to make decisions as early as age two. For example, he would put two different kinds of cereal on the table in front of her and ask, "Which kind of cereal do you want, honey?" Or, I would show her two different sets of clothes and ask, "Which outfit would you like to wear today?" Both options were appropriate choices, yet we were giving our young daughter an opportunity to practice making a decision.

As she grew older, I would introduce a different learning situation by giving her the option to wear a cold weather outfit or a sundress to school on a given day. If it was a hot day, and she chose the cooler outfit, I would ask her to explain why she made that choice. If children can put their thought process into words (very difficult at a young age), the experience becomes a lesson. When we give our kids small opportunities for independence when they are young, and provide them with increased independence and responsibility as the years go by, we are helping them learn to be faithful as well as trustworthy. We see this principle in Luke 16:10, which says, "Whoever can be trusted with very little can also be trusted with much, and whoever is dishonest with very little will also be dishonest with much." Drawing your children's attention to this verse helps them understand that faithfulness, trustworthiness, and responsibility are not just characteristics of maturity, they are spiritual principles.

Of course, it's possible to take this principle too far, and some parents do. We have to keep a balance by not giving so much freedom that our kids are unprotected and vulnerable. For example, a mom who has become so preoccupied with work or a favorite hobby might allow her children to play outside unattended for hours at a time, saying, "but we live in such a nice neighborhood, and the dog would bark if there was trouble." You should also beware of falling into the "what do you want for dinner" trap. Don't make special meals for a child if he or she doesn't want to eat what you've prepared. Parents who do this are allowing the child to become the authority in the home.

*Allow your kids to make mistakes and suffer the natural con-
sequences in a safe environment where they can analyze their
thoughts, discover what went wrong, correct their thinking and the
situation, and learn from their mistakes.* Mistakes can be used
to teach important life lessons. God designed us perfectly, but
not perfect.

What kind of mistakes is it okay to let kids make?

In general, I don't intervene unless the natural consequence
of the poor choice is one that threatens the physical, emotional,
or spiritual well-being of my child. So if Becky chooses to wear
a warm outfit on a hot day, she is going to suffer the natural
consequence of getting overheated. When she wants to change
into something cooler, I can help her analyze her thinking and I
can also help her reason through the situation the next time.

Here are some other "safe mistakes" children might make
(and the consequence). I recommend that you allow these mistakes *once*. Then follow up the consequences with teaching about
what went wrong and what to do better the next time.

Younger kids:

- Eating too much candy (he gets a tummy ache)
- "Losing" a library book under her bed (she pays a fine)
- Choosing ugly sneakers at the store (he has to wear them)

Older kids:

- Talking too long on the phone (she pays for the extra
  minutes)
- Turning in a school project late (he gets a lower grade)
- Forgetting sneakers for gym class (she has to attend a
  make up class)

It's so much easier, quicker, and safer to make all of your children's decisions. However, if you fall into this trap, how will they know how to make responsible choices as adults?

As hard as it sounds, don't rescue your children. Let's say it was your daughter who forgot her gym shoes, which means she'll miss class and have to make it up the next day. What would you do if she called you and asked you to run them over to her in time for gym? If you do as she asked, you'd be "rescuing" her. Occasionally rescuing is okay, but most times it's better if kids have to suffer the natural consequences. That's how they learn. When your children suffer a painful, natural consequence of a poor choice, stand *with* them, but don't stand up *for* them. Let them learn to stand up for themselves, taking responsibility for their own actions.

That's what one mom I know did. Her teenage son was arrested for committing a small crime. Because this was the first time he had done anything like this, she bailed him out. However, when it happened again, she refused to bail him out—*but she sat with him for the length of his short incarceration.* This wise mom allowed her son to suffer the natural consequences of his actions. She didn't rescue him, but she was there with him through the ordeal. Her actions demonstrated God's unconditional love for us.

Of course, when we let go of our kids, we are trusting them to make wise decisions—scary! More importantly, we are trusting *God* with our children. Trust in God is the key to the concept of letting go. How much do you know about Him?

Trusting God

Would you trust a stranger with your precious child? We tend to trust only people whom we know, people with a proven track record of faithfulness. So it is with God. The more we know of

God, the more we can trust Him. The bigger our picture of God, the greater will be our ability to trust Him. The smaller our God, the less trustworthy He seems.

Are you willing to entrust your children to Him? Do you trust Him enough? You can enlarge your understanding of God by doing the following things:

- Spend time with Him every day and walk with Him throughout the day, noticing Him in everything you see and everything that happens.
- Commit to praying with a prayer partner who will hold you accountable and help you see what God is doing in your life and in the world around you through answered prayer.
- Partner with your children to learn more about God by having devotions together every morning or evening, going on God Hunts, and studying the Bible together.

Hebrews 11:6 tells us, "without faith [trust] it is impossible to please God, because anyone who comes to him must believe that he exists and that he rewards those who earnestly seek him." Without the existence of God, where is hope? But "with God all things are possible" (Matthew 19:26).

Solomon, the wisest man who ever lived, said, "He who trusts in himself is a fool, but he who walks in wisdom is kept safe" (Proverbs 28:26). Are you walking in God's wisdom, or are you still in the driver's seat? The parent's version of Proverbs 3:5-6 could go something like this: "Trust in the Lord with all your heart and do not count on your own parenting skills and wisdom. In all your parenting, you must acknowledge God—and He will help you to be the parent your child needs."

When we feel out of control, it's not the time to hold on to our kids more tightly—it's time to turn control over to the One who sustains the universe. I make it my goal every day to turn control of my life over to Him before I even start the day (the "Y" in P-R-A-Y stands for "yield"). When I trust the sovereign God to work in my heart and in my daughter's heart, I am able to trust Him with the outcome.

Is there any guarantee that our children will follow after their heavenly Father instead of their earthly one? Try as we might to help others, we cannot make the decision for them. Yes, we can exemplify God's truth to others, influence them to a degree, and pray for them. But all the while, we must hold our loved ones in an open hand.

Is there really any choice but to trust God with our children? In the absence of a human father's godly leadership and teaching, we *must* rely on their heavenly Father. In the day in which we live, our children need to learn to be "as shrewd as snakes and as innocent as doves" (Matthew 10:16), which comes through an intimate, one-on-one relationship with the almighty God.

And He is worthy:

> *As for God, his way is perfect;*
> *the word of the LORD is flawless.*
> *He is a shield*
> *for all who take refuge in him.*
> *For who is God besides the LORD?*
> *And who is the Rock except our God?*
> *It is God who arms me with strength*
> *and makes my way perfect.*
>
> 2 Samuel 22:31-33

God can also make your child's way perfect—perfect according to *His* plan, sovereignty, and strength.

Strength

> *Trust in the LORD with all your heart*
> *and lean not on your own understanding;*
> *in all your ways acknowledge him,*
> *and he will make your paths straight.*
>
> Proverbs 3:5-6

Strategies

- We can so desperately desire our children to love God that we push Him right down their throats.
- Unless you give your kids freedom to make choices—and mistakes—they most likely won't develop the necessary skills to make wise decisions in the future.
- Mistakes are good tools for learning important lessons.
- The practice of letting go begins right now—trusting your children with little things.
- By deliberately pushing your children "out of the nest" little by little, you practice the valuable principles of letting go and trusting God.
- Hold your children in an open hand, trusting them to God.
- The bigger your picture of God, the greater will be your ability to trust Him.

Self-Assessment

1. How can mistakes be a positive part of your child's life?
2. Before asking yourself if you trust God, ask, *Do I know Him?* How big is your picture of God?

3. How do you react when your authority, schedule, or ideas are challenged? Are you able to let go of your own thinking, step back and look at the big picture, and accept a new way of thinking?

4. To what extent are you willing to trust God?

5. What is trust? Where does it come from? Where does it go? How do you get it back?

6. Do you remember how you felt on your children's first day of kindergarten? Why did you feel this way?

7. How are you holding your children—in a hand opened flat, in a hand with fingers slightly curled, or in a hand clutched tightly into a fist? Explain your answer.

8. What is the hardest part of trusting and letting go for you? Why?

Speaking with God

O faithful God,
I praise you for never, ever forsaking me.
I repent of fear, doubt, distrust, and manipulation.
Please increase my faith and teach me
how and when to release my children to you.
I yield myself to your sovereignty and faithfulness.

Chapter 12
Crossing the Finish Line

When Becky came home recently with her school report card, I began to wonder what my progress report would look like if God graded mothers. In my mind, God gave me a picture of my parenting report card, but I could not see the actual grades I had earned because over every letter was an "A+" written in Jesus' blood. With unconditional love, God is helping me—and you—be everything He created a mother to be.

Here are three truths I hope and pray you take away from this book:

1. Long ago God perfectly designed you to mother your unique children (see Ephesians 2:10).
2. He knows what every day holds years before it happens (see Psalm 139:16).
3. He will provide the strength for you to accomplish what He has called you to do (see 1 Thessalonians 5:24).

How well are we applying these truths to our lives? I've deliberately used the pronoun *we* because I'm not done learning or growing either, and I still make mistakes and get frustrated. That's why I'm constantly asking myself questions such as the following. As you read through them, answer each question for yourself.

How am I dealing with my own needs? Am I content with my lot in life? How do I measure up and what do I have to work on in the areas of the spiritual, emotional, mental, physical, and social aspects of my life? How are my priorities? Have I cleaned up my thinking?

Am I seeking to understand and love the unique people God placed in my family? Am I connecting with my family? How is my timing and attitude when I communicate with my child (and my husband)? Am I honest? Encouraging? Am I lovingly respecting my husband? Is God helping me answer my child's tough questions? Can she see Jesus in me now more than ever?

Have I tackled the tasks of spiritually single mothering with new energy? How well am I able to control my child when her self-discipline slips? Have I built up a support system of godly encouragers — and am I using it? Where and how is my family serving the Lord? Am I trusting God in the big and small details of life and mothering? Am I appropriately releasing and relinquishing my child to God's wise care and continued intervention?

God judges each of us on our own actions, attitudes, and conversation. Although the world may judge you far differently, God does not judge you based on the behavior of your children, but on your own trust and obedience. If you are walking closely with your Savior day by day and your life reflects God to your children, you've passed. Your children will be judged on what they did with the God you introduced to them — you are not responsible for what they do with Him, nor do you get the credit. Whatever good marks we receive on our spiritual report card truly belong to the God who enables us to do anything good and positive in this life. It is only by His grace that we live and move and have our being (see Acts 17:28).

Only God knows how long you will be alone in your desire and efforts to help your children love God. Your husband may soon see the Light—or he may choose not to look at God until he's forced to face Him in the next life. Regardless of how long it takes, living spiritually single takes a toll. Please, dear one, in your desperation to love and be loved, do not place inappropriate emphasis on your relationship with your children or your hopes for them.

Each precious child *belongs* to God. Although God gifted you with the honor of being a child's mother, the child is not yours. God entrusted this child to you for his or her formative years. Enjoy and treasure the years you have together, but be mindful that the child is not *your* treasure—he or she is simply on loan.

And do your task of mothering to the glory of God. Then, one day in the not-so-distant future, you will hear God say, "Well done, good and faithful servant!" (Matthew 25:21). For now, God is whispering:

> *"My dear child,*
> *although it defies your comprehension,*
> *I love your children*
> *infinitely more than you do.*
> *And I promise, throughout their lives on earth,*
> *I will woo them with my Shepherd's heart.*
> *Trust me. Rest in me. Glorify me.*
> *I have created you and each of your children,*
> *and I have placed these children in your home because*

you are the perfect mother for these children.
No, dear one, you are not perfect
but have been perfectly chosen to be the mother of these
little ones I love.
Stay confident in your faith, and persevere,
for in just a very little while I will come, and say,
'Well done, good and faithful servant!'
I give you my unending love and all the provisions you need."

Appendix

Becky Meyer's Standards and Convictions for Her Teen Years

November 15, 2003 — Thirteenth Birthday

Note: I've placed this list here in order to illustrate what your child can come up with as you work with him or her to develop a set of standards and convictions for how to live as a teenager. Becky and I spent several hours looking through Christian books and magazines together, making notes about what others believe. Then we went to the Bible to find actual verses that state what God says. I was the catalyst, guide, and encourager, but she made final decisions and did the typing — so she "owns" these beliefs.

My beliefs about God:

God alone is the eternal God:

> *Before the mountains were born*
> *or you brought forth the earth and the world,*
> *from everlasting to everlasting you are God.*
>
> Psalm 90:2

God is sovereign and has absolute authority:

> *Everyone must submit himself to the governing*
> *authorities, for there is no authority except that*
> *which God has established. The authorities that exist*
> *have been established by God.*
>
> Romans 13:1

God loves us, and each of us is a person of value:

> *I have been crucified with Christ and I no longer*
> *live, but Christ lives in me. The life I live in the*
> *body, I live by faith in the Son of God, who loved me*
> *and gave Himself for me.*
>
> Galatians 2:20

Jesus Christ must be my Savior and Lord:

> *If you confess with your mouth, 'Jesus is Lord,' and*
> *believe in your heart that God raised him from the*
> *dead, you will be saved.*
>
> Romans 10:9

God's Word, the Bible, is our infallible standard for faith and obedience. Those who resist its authority will be blown off course by their own feelings and cultural trends; *veritas* (truth):

> *All Scripture is God-breathed and is useful for teaching, rebuking, correcting and training in righteousness, so that the man of God may be thoroughly equipped for every good work.*
>
> 2 Timothy 3:16

Application of God's principles is impossible apart from the Holy Spirit. While we must participate in change, He is the source of our power:

> *"The Counselor, the Holy Spirit, whom the Father will send in my name, will teach you all things and will remind you of everything I have said to you."*
>
> John 14:26

God is faithful to me:

> *The one who calls you is faithful and he will do it.*
>
> 1 Thessalonians 5:24

God will never leave me:

> *God has said,*
> *"Never will I leave you;*
> *never will I forsake you."*
> *So we say with confidence,*

*"The Lord is my helper; I will not be afraid.
What can man do to me?"*

Hebrews 13:5-6

My convictions regarding myself:

Regular prayer must be a crucial part of my daily life:

*Devote yourselves to prayer, being watchful and
thankful.*

Colossians 4:2

1. *Praise:*

*I will extol the LORD at all times;
    his praise will always be on my lips.*

Psalm 34:1

2. *Repent:*

*If we confess our sins, he is faithful and just and
will forgive us our sins and purify us from all
unrighteousness.*

John 1:9

3. *Ask:*

*"You may ask me for anything in my name, and I
will do it."*

John 14:14

4. *Yield:*

> *Yet, O LORD, you are our Father.*
> *We are the clay, you are the potter;*
> *we are all the work of your hand.*

Isaiah 64:8

The Scriptures are God's Word and serve as my daily guide:

> *Your word is a lamp to my feet*
> *and a light for my path.*

Psalm 119:105

I will trust God in everything:

> *Trust in the LORD with all your heart*
> *and lean not on your own understanding;*
> *in all your ways acknowledge him,*
> *and he will make your paths straight.*

Proverbs 3:5-6

I will obey and love God always; *semper fidelis* (always faithful):

> *This is love for God: to obey his commands.*

1 John 5:3

I will work to the best of my ability in everything I do, to God's glory; *ad optimum ingeni* (to the best of my ability):

> *And whatever you do, whether in word or deed, do*
> *it all in the name of the Lord Jesus, giving thanks to*

God the Father through him.

Colossians 3:17

I will confess my sins frequently and keep short accounts; *tabula rasa* (clean slate):

> *"In your anger do not sin": Do not let the sun go down while you are still angry, and do not give the devil a foothold.*

Ephesians 4:26-27

I will reject the world's thinking by deliberately thinking godly thoughts:

> *Do not conform any longer to the pattern of this world, but be transformed by the renewing of your mind. Then you will be able to test and approve what God's will is — his good, pleasing and perfect will.*

Romans 12:2

I will fear nothing but the almighty God of creation:

> *For God hath not given us the spirit of fear; but of power, and of love, and of a sound mind.*

2 Timothy 1:7, KJV

I will manage my time wisely and make every God-given moment count; *carpe diem* (seize the day):

> *Go to the ant, you sluggard;*
> *consider its ways and be wise!*

Proverbs 6:6

I will give regularly to the Lord's work:

> *Each man should give what he has decided in his heart to give, not reluctantly or under compulsion, for God loves a cheerful giver.*
>
> 2 Corinthians 9:7

I will be pure in my appearance, my words, and my actions because the world is watching:

> *Therefore as God's chosen people, holy and dearly loved, clothe yourselves with compassion, kindness, humility, gentleness and patience.*
>
> Colossians 3:12

I will reserve the high places of honor in my heart for believers only:

> *Do not be yoked together with unbelievers. For what do righteousness and wickedness have in common? Or what fellowship can light have with darkness?*
>
> 2 Corinthians 6:14

My convictions regarding others:

I will be discerning, not judgmental of others:

> *"Do not judge, or you too will be judged. For in the same way you judge others, you will be judged."*
>
> Matthew 7:1-2

Nancy Sebastian Meyer

I will always be prepared to graciously respond to questions about my faith:

> But in your hearts set apart Christ as Lord. Always
> be prepared to give an answer to everyone who asks
> you to give the reason for the hope that you have. But
> do this with gentleness and respect.
>
> 1 Peter 3:15

I will be humble and give more thought to others than to myself:

> Do nothing out of selfish ambition or vain
> conceit, but in humility consider others better than
> yourselves.
>
> Philippians 2:3

I will not let anyone's opinions or persecution sway my decision to glorify God always:

> Don't let anyone look down on you because you are
> young, but set an example for the believers in speech,
> in life, in love, in faith and in purity.
>
> 1 Timothy 4:12

I will worship and fellowship with believers regularly:

> And let us consider how we may spur one another
> on toward love and good deeds. Let us not give up
> meeting together, as some are in the habit of doing,

*but let us encourage one another — and all the more
as you see the Day approaching.*

Hebrews 10:24-25

These are my personal standards and convictions, and I will live them out by God's grace.

Signed: *Rebecca Lindsay Meyer*

1. Taken from *You Are Special* by Max Lucado, copyright© 1997, edited by Karen Hill. Used by permission of Crossway Books, a publishing ministry of Good News Publishers, Wheaton, IL 60187. For more information, visit www.crossway.com.

2. David Murrow, *Why Men Hate Going to Church* (Nashville, TN: Nelson, 2005), 72.

3. Murrow, 51.

4. Murrow, 196-202.

5. Rick Warren, *The Purpose Driven Life* (Grand Rapids, MI: Zondervan, 2002), 90.

6. Henry T. Blackaby and Claude V. King, *Experiencing God* (Nashville, TN: Lifeway Press, 1990), 67.

7. Betty N. Chase, *Discipline Them, Love Them* (Elgin, IL: David C. Cook Publishing, 1993), 92-94.

For Further Reading

Chapman, Gary D., and Ross Campbell, M.D. *The Five Love Languages of Children*. Chicago: Northfield Publishing, 1997.

Chase, Betty N. *Discipline Them, Love Them*. Elgin, IL: David C. Cook Publishing, 1982.

Cloud, Dr. Henry, and Dr. John Townsend. *Boundaries with Kids*. Grand Rapids, MI: Zondervan, 1998.

Dillow, Linda. *Creative Counterpart: Becoming the Woman, Wife, and Mother You've Longed to Be*. Nashville: Thomas Nelson, 1977.

Freeman, Becky. *Milk and Cookies to Make You Smile*. Eugene, OR: Harvest House, 2002.

Littauer, Florence. *Personality Plus for Parents: Understanding What Makes Your Child Tick*. Grand Rapids, MI: Fleming H. Revell, 2000.

Littauer, Florence. *Your Personality Tree*. Dallas: Word, 1986.

McGee, Robert S. *The Search for Significance*. Nashville: W Publishing, 1998.

Trent, John, Ph.D., Rick Osborne, and Kurt Bruner. *Parent's Guide to the Spiritual Growth of Children: Helping Your Child Develop a Personal Faith*. Focus on the Family. Wheaton, IL: Tyndale, 2000.

Married for more than twenty-two years to her college sweet-heart, Nancy has spent more than half that time as a spiritually single mom. Rich, a pastor-turned-agnostic, supports her ministry to wives and moms saying, "If you can help women hang on in difficult relationships in order to keep families together, share what you need to about us."

Nancy is an inspirational speaker, recording artist, and author of several books, including *Beyond Expectations: Finding Joy In Your Marriage* (Moody, 2003) and *Talk Easy, Listen Hard: Real Communication for Two Really Different People* (Moody, 2006). Her ministry, *Hope4Hearts*, offers God's hope to the hearts of wives, women, moms, and children. One of Nancy's greatest joys is ministering with her teenage daughter, Becky, at mother-daughter events, conferences, and retreats.

Nancy, Rich, and Becky live in Lancaster, Pennsylvania. A voracious reader, Nancy loves to relax with a good book or discuss a recent favorite with a good friend over a cup of Chai.

Contact Nancy through her website
www.hope4hearts.net
or by writing to
Hope 4 Hearts
PO Box 10062
Lancaster, PA 17605-0062.

INSPIRING BOOKS TO HELP YOU THROUGH THE TOUGH TIMES.

Donkeys Still Talk

Virelle Kidder   1-57683-460-3

Sometimes the difficult people and challenging circumstances in our lives are God's attempt to get our attention. See how He still uses the "donkeys" in our lives to make His personal messages to us known.

On Our Own

Lela Gilbert   1-60006-101-X

Today's single moms are finding it increasingly difficult to juggle the demands of a full-time job, raising their children, and finding time for themselves. Focusing on core areas such as finances, legal issues, and new relationships, author Lela Gilbert provides practical guidance and a welcome dose of hope and encouragement.

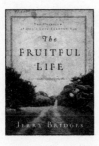

The Fruitful Life

Jerry Bridges   1-60006-027-7

As we become serious followers of Christ, we want to live loving, joyful, anxiety-free lives. This book will guide you on that quest by focusing on God's nature as revealed in Scripture and by helping you cultivate the beautiful fruit given by the Holy Spirit.

To order copies, visit your local Christian bookstore, call NavPress at 1-800-366-7788, or log on to www.navpress.com.
To locate a Christian bookstore near you, call 1-800-991-7747.

NAVPRESS®
BRINGING TRUTH TO LIFE
www.navpress.com